Seasons in My Life

By Geneva Servais

ISBN: 978-0-578-60425-1

Contents

"We are thrilled to find out that Geneva Servais has finally put her enthralling story to paper. Before we ever met Geneva and her husband, Ted, in person, we had heard about their noteworthy kindness, generosity, and passion for the Lord.

Then about ten years ago, Brian and I had the privilege of getting to know Ted and Geneva ourselves, and found that the rumors about their kindness, generosity, and passion for Jesus were all true. It was then that Geneva shared some of the highlights of her story with me, beginning sometime before World War 2, scanning the events of Southern California history, and reaching to the present.

Within her chronicle is tragedy, intrigue, hard work, and the wonder working providence of God. This is a story worth reading even as Geneva is a person worth knowing!!!!"

— Cheryl Brodersen ~ Speaker, Author, and Director of Joyful Living Women's Ministry at Calvary Chapel Costa Mesa

Dedication

I dedicate this book to Pastor Greg and Cathe Laurie, who stepped up and had "ears to hear" when I asked if they would help me do this book. Greg's own book *Tell Someone*, given to me at Harvest America in 2016, is what prompted me to ask them, and I pray that many would be blessed as a result of this book.

Thank you, Greg and Cathe.
We are forever thankful to you both.

To everything there is a season,
A time for every purpose under heaven:
A time to be born,
And a time to die;
A time to plant,
And a time to pluck what is planted;
A time to kill,
And a time to heal;
A time to break down,
And a time to build up;
A time to weep,
And a time to laugh;
A time to mourn,
And a time to dance;
A time to cast away stones,
And a time to gather stones;
A time to embrace,
And a time to refrain from embracing;
A time to gain,
And a time to lose;
A time to keep,
And a time to throw away;
A time to tear,
And a time to sew;
A time to keep silence,
And a time to speak;
A time to love,
And a time to hate;
A time of war,
And a time of peace.

—*Ecclesiastes 3:1–8*

Foreword

I love stories.

I've always been captivated by a good story … a compelling story … an inspiring story. Jesus Himself frequently used stories to draw in His listeners and convey the profound truths that God wanted them to hear.

In addition to writing my own story, I've written two biographies about two very unique people: actor Steve McQueen and singer Johnny Cash. The story you are about to read—Geneva's story—is far different from theirs in almost every way, except the one that counts the most: all three of these amazing stories point to the greatest story ever told—the story of Jesus Christ.

Born six years before McQueen and eight years before Cash, Geneva has outlived them both by decades. Now in her mid-nineties, she shows every indication of outliving them for many more years to come. Like Cash, Geneva spent much of her early life thinking she was closer to God than she really was. And like McQueen, she made her commitment to follow Jesus much later in life than most people do.

But unlike Cash and McQueen, Geneva is no celebrity. It's unlikely that you have ever heard her name or seen her face. That hasn't stopped her from using her influence and her resources to do God's work. In fact, I wouldn't be surprised if in the end, more people have been spiritually impacted through the ministry of Geneva and her husband, Ted, than that of McQueen and Cash combined.

Among many other things, God has bestowed on Geneva and Ted an amazing ability, capacity, and propensity to *give*. Blessing their business endeavors, God has used the Servaises as a conduit of His grace. Their faithful, consistent, abundant support of dozens of evangelical ministries has helped to fund God's work all over the world, and untold thousands of people have been introduced to the gospel because of their willingness to be used by Him.

Geneva and Ted have a heart for people, and they recognize that the time is now to spread the Good News of Jesus Christ as far and wide as they can, while they can. I can't think of a more worthwhile legacy to leave.

As you'll soon read, Geneva has encountered some very trying and surprising episodes in her life, as well as many blessings and good times. As Solomon so wisely wrote thousands of years ago, "To everything there is a season, a time for every purpose under Heaven." I'm grateful to God that He has allowed Geneva to experience so many seasons in her life, and that she has generously shared the lessons she's learned from those seasons—as freely and as cheerfully as she shares her time, her resources, and her testimony. May God use this book to bless others and draw them closer to Him!

Greg Laurie

Pastor and Evangelist, Harvest Ministries

Introduction

To everything there is a season, a time for every purpose under heaven.

> *"And now that I am old and gray, don't forsake me. Give me time to tell this new generation (and their children too) about all your mighty miracles. Your power and goodness, Lord, reach to the highest heavens. You have done such wonderful things. Where is there another God like you? You have let me sink down deep in desperate problems. But you will bring me back to life again, up from the depths of the earth. You will give me greater honor than before and turn again and comfort me."*
>
> *—Psalm 71:18–21 TLB*

For many years now I have wanted to write a book and have been told by many people that I should do so. I once asked a pastor friend, David Wilkerson, what he thought about the idea and his advice was the best I could have received at the time. He said, "We will lift you up in prayer and when the Lord wants you to write it, you will know."

Since 1958, off and on, I would start to write, but

I always tabled it, as the timing just didn't seem right. That is, until 2016, when Pastor Greg Laurie of Harvest Ministries was doing a crusade in Dallas, Texas, at AT&T Stadium. Through that crusade, I received a book called *Tell Someone*, and that was my cue. I knew it was time.

You see, back in the 1950s when the idea first arose, I hadn't begun to have enough to write about. I thought I had, but there were so many more experiences to go through—both good and bad. Now, decades later, I can look back on the seasons in my life and draw wisdom from my experiences to share with others.

First and foremost, the purpose of this book is to show how God has been at work throughout my life—through thick and thin, up and down. It has been a wonderful journey and I wouldn't change a thing.

Each chapter of this book represents a lesson God has helped me to learn. While some people may not have been challenged with the same lessons I have, others have been through so much more! I do not want to focus on my trials but to share instead how the Lord has walked right alongside me the whole way. I want to tell you what He has done for me and through me. The Bible says that if you are going to boast about anything, then boast about the Lord (1 Corinthians 1:31) and that is what I intend to do!

A Time To Be Born

In 1924, my dad was working for Griffith Company when they started to dredge the bay and form Lido Island in Newport Beach, California. When it was completed, the company was hard pressed to sell lots, as no one wanted to buy land on a sand fill! The company owed my dad six hundred dollars for his work and instead of paying him, they offered him two lots on the east end of the island, which is now called the "Gold Coast."

He answered their offer with the same words as everyone else: "Why in the world would I want that?" He had a baby coming and he needed cash, so he turned it down.

I was that baby, and those two lots are worth millions today!

Yes, I was born in 1924 in the city of Pasadena, which means that at the time of writing this book, I am ninety-five years young. I'm still driving a little, cooking (such as it is), doing laundry, shopping at the market, and doing a little bit of travel. I consider my current mobility and capability a huge blessing.

Growing up, I had three siblings. First was my sister, two years older, whose name was Drusilla. Next was my brother Teddy, who was three years younger. And finally, my brother Jerry, seven years younger, was the baby of the family.

Drusilla and I were very close. We did everything together and had friends that we shared who lived close by. My grandmother would make matching dresses for Drusilla and me, so we were often mistaken for twins. She and I both loved music; she would play the piano and I would sing.

Brother Teddy was a quiet, happy little guy. You could give him some toys on the floor and he would play with them all day! We got along really well together. As he grew up, he liked to sing, and so did I. Music was the direction we both pursued. He sang in the John Henry Lyons boys' choir when we lived in Pasadena, as well as in a choir in Big Bear later on.

Teddy and I used to walk along the lakeside in Big Bear, finding little garter snakes, as well as turquoise and yellow striped skinks. We would put them in jars and take them to school to share. We grew up very close and had a special relationship of caring for each other.

Jerry, on the other hand, was always into things,

inquisitive, and busy. Our relationship was more distant, probably because he was so much younger, and we had less in common.

I had a pretty normal life as a child, going to school and playing with neighborhood friends. We did a lot of roller skating and stayed busy all the time. Drusilla and I went to St. Phillip's Catholic School through the third grade. After that, we went to public school: Webster Elementary, John Marshall Junior High, and later, Pasadena Junior College.

In our early years, Dad had his own excavating business. It was wartime—blackout drapes, curfews, food rationing, and our loved ones off to fight! Those were hard years. It was especially hard for Mom, who was used to having everything she needed or wanted. With food rationing, we were always running out of butter, flour, and sugar—always trying to make things go further to survive. We learned to trade food stamps or exchange scarce food with others just to get by. (I still have food stamps left from those years!)

President Roosevelt established the Works Progress Administration (WPA) to employ millions of men to build roads and buildings, so there were plenty of projects and jobs for my dad to work on.

Dad had his own equipment and dug many of the basements for the buildings along Colorado Street in Pasadena, the City Hall, and Caltech. He did most of the sidewalks too. Some places still have his name on them. I remember when we girls were about eight and ten, we got to ride in the trucks as they hauled the dirt out to Brookside Park and the Rose Bowl area before they were built.

With all that work, I guess Dad was "sitting pretty" financially. He must have made good money as we had a nanny for years and we loved her. I was just reading a birthday card she sent to me years after I was married. She wrote a special note that said, "You were only two years old when I came to stay with you little rascals. I have such good memories, and you four children were the best little ones I ever took care of." I appreciated her staying in touch with me and having said that so long ago.

We used to go out to dinner as a family to the Good Fellows Grill (with tablecloths and everything!) and Mom always told us we had to "take our good manners with us." All in all, I would say I had a good homelife and childhood.

The Bible reminds us, "Whatever is good and perfect is a gift coming down to us from God our Father" (James 1:17 NLT). God's provision, His protection, and life itself are all gifts that we so often take for granted, don't we? The older I get, the more I realize how precious and valuable His blessings are. It's only right that we respond with a heart of gratitude and thanksgiving for all that He has given.

A Time of Peace

Some of my favorite memories from childhood include playing baseball in the middle of the street in front of the house. You could do that in those days without any danger. The street was extra wide and not many cars went by. One neighboring house had nine children, another had two, and our home had four, so we always had enough kids for a baseball team.

I remember my grandma would come to visit and we would read the Bible and go to church on Sundays. She came during the summer and she taught me how to sew old material cutouts together and make quilts. Grandma would sit by the fire with us and tell us stories of her and Grandpa Ducey in their young life.

I also remember Mom teaching me how to bake—cakes, cobblers, and lemon meringue pies. Mom always knew exactly how much wood to put in the wood stove to make perfect meringues. We kids would play board games, like Chinese Checkers and

Monopoly, and we would read stories such as Nancy Drew and Dick Tracy.

As we grew older, one of our first jobs was collecting papers. It was during the time of World War II and they paid us good money for the papers we collected. Teddy, Jerry, and I would knock on doors and collect the papers while Drusilla drove the car.

After school and on Saturdays, we would take the back seat out of the car, fill it with the papers we collected from nearby neighborhoods, and drive it to the paper mill. There they would weigh our car, take the papers out, and then weigh the car again. We would get paid according to the weight of the papers we brought. We did that over and over again.

I was my dad's buddy, and a tomboy, if you will. Dad was always so good to me and I loved him. He had a kayak that he would use to go duck hunting, and sometimes he would take me along with him. We would go early in the morning while it was still dark, and he would almost always catch his limit of ducks. I didn't go along when he hunted bigger game. He knew I liked animals so he often would bring something home for me from a job, like a baby rabbit or a tarantula. My favorite was a baby lamb, white with a black spot on its eye.

You've heard the nursery rhyme about Mary's little lamb who went wherever Mary went and followed her to school. Well, my little lamb followed me everywhere too, but mine went into the grocery store. Back then, no one would mind such a thing—that is, until one day my lamb piddled on the floor as we were going through the check stand. The manager handed me a rag, asked me to wipe it up, and said, "Please leave your lamb home from now on."

Dad made a large aviary in the backyard for raising canaries and parakeets. He also fenced off the back half of the yard for all kinds of animals: chickens, ducks, pigeons, squabs, and pheasants. I remember Dad building a double fishpond in the backyard; we kept goldfish in it.

We had dogs as well: a cocker spaniel, Boston terriers, and Scotties. We raised puppies and sold them, so we always had pets around. It was a very good thing for us, as it taught us to be responsible and it gave us a love for animals.

My dad taught us a lot of valuable skills as well. For instance, he showed me how to butcher all of the animals that he would hunt. Later, when I went to work at a grocery store and spent time in the meat department, the men were amazed at how fast I "caught on" to their instruction about how to make the different cuts. I never told them my secret; I just let them believe I was a really fast learner! (Decades later, after my father passed away, I was fine to sell most of the antiques and possessions from the home, but I cried when I parted with Dad's butcher block.)

I was always a "good girl," but at some point I had done something wrong (I can't remember what it was), so when Dad came home, he took me into the bedroom, put me over his lap, and paddled me with a hairbrush. I can still feel the hurt in my heart because he had to do that. It was the only paddling I can remember, as I didn't want that to happen again!

It seems to me as I look back, my mom and I were not very close. She was a loving mom and caring, always doing things with us. I remember coloring eggs with her and making up baskets together to give to our school friends. But she was the disciplinarian and always had jobs for me. I mowed the lawn, trimmed the hedges, washed the windows, cleaned the oriental rugs on my hands and knees with ammonia water, cleaned the fishpond, fed the animals and cleaned up after them, picked the peaches and figs—many, many jobs. Of course, I would rather have been playing baseball or roller skating.

I didn't like doing them at the time, but I'm glad now that I had to do so many chores and jobs. It established a good work ethic in me and taught me how to be productive with my time. The Bible says, "A hard worker has plenty of food, but a person who chases fantasies has no sense" (Proverbs 12:11 NLT), and also "Work brings profit, but mere talk leads to poverty" (Proverbs 14:23 NLT). I would continue to work hard into my adult life as a result of that early training, and I would see God's blessings as a result.

3

A Time To Mourn

When Drusilla was fifteen, she ended up bedridden for three years. It began with appendicitis. While in the hospital, she came down with strep throat, which turned into rheumatic fever and went downhill from there.

Not knowing much about medical things, Mom and Dad tried everything they heard about to help her get better. For a while, Drusilla did get better and went back to school. But one day, when there was flooding, Drusilla got her feet wet and they stayed wet all throughout her day at school. That dragged her back down into illness, so back to bed she went, this time with more complications.

The doctors worked hard to treat her, but to no avail. In 1940, when I was sixteen, Drusilla passed away. It was so hard on Mom during that final time to not be able to help her. Mom did what she could to make Drusilla comfortable, but knew she was not going to get better.

Losing Drusilla was a sorrowful time for our family. In every life, there are times of mourning, when we grieve the loss of someone or something. Jesus said, "Blessed are those who mourn, for they will be comforted." Although we were professing Catholics at the time, I didn't have a close personal relationship with Jesus Christ. It wouldn't be until later that I would truly understand and appreciate the comfort that God offers us in times of mourning.

4

A Time of War

My dad had a bad leg for most of his life. When he was twelve years old and automobiles first came on the scene, he was standing on a sidewalk and a car went by. Its tire hit a rock in the street, causing the rock to fly up and hit my dad in the leg. It splintered his shinbone. He had an open sore that wouldn't heal.

Every once in a while, it would flare up, so Mom boiled towels on the stove and we girls would take turns putting them on his leg. These hot compresses would release the pressure and give him some relief until the next time.

At the end of 1941, my dad was recovering from surgery on his leg at the Huntington Memorial Hospital in Pasadena. He was a ham radio operator and an expert in Morse code.

On December 7, while convalescing from his surgery, he was listening to the Morse code signals on his ham radio and overheard a message that Pearl Harbor had been attacked!

He quickly called the nurse and told her, "War just broke out in Pearl Harbor, so go tell the doctor. You'd better let everybody know about it." So she went and told the doctor, but the doctor, thinking he was still out of it from his surgery or medication, simply told the nurse, "Put the railings up on his bed" so he wouldn't fall out of bed in his delirium. Nobody believed what Dad was telling them.

About two hours later, when the mainstream news finally broadcast that war had broken out in Pearl Harbor, all of the nurses and doctors started coming into my dad's room to hear what he had to say from his radio. Suddenly he was the expert!

That's a funny and light little story from a heavier time in history, but it demonstrates the fact that people don't always want to hear the truth. When life is comfortable and war seems far away, it's easy to close your ears to a message of danger. The same is true spiritually speaking. Some people are so comfortable in their lifestyle that they close their ears to the gospel message and God's offer of salvation from sin. Sometimes God allows unexpected circumstances to wake us up and bring us back to reality.

5

A Time To Build Up

School was hard for me. English and math didn't come easy. But I loved every bit of singing and soon I was singing for my girlfriends' weddings. I then started professional singing lessons as the teacher thought I had promise of a good future.

When my sister became ill, everything changed. I still held onto music but stopped the private lessons. I majored in music at Pasadena Junior College, and it was there that I fell in love with a fellow music student and became engaged.

We had great fun going to campfires on the beach, and singing with our whole choral group, which was what we liked to do. But soon the young man I was engaged to was drafted into the Air Force and was sent off to Germany.

He was gone for over a year, and when he came home, he was a different person. While he was away, our family had moved to Big Bear, California. Since things had changed between us and because of the distance, that romance came to an end.

When we moved to Big Bear, the cabin we moved into needed a lot of work, so Dad dove right in. He had a well dug so we finally had our own fresh water, and then came the electricity. No more eating by candlelight or hauling our water five miles in big jugs.

The cabin had a one-car garage beneath it, but Dad was able to widen that space to make room for another car, as well as build out a workshop and a storage room for preserves and pantry items. We always called that the "goodie room." He did all of it by scraping the dirt under the house with a pick and shovel, then putting it into a bucket. He would shore up the house as he dug out more and more space beneath it. Instead of just throwing the dirt out to pile up in front of the garage, he thought it would be more useful behind the house. So he sawed a hole in the floor of a closet and set up a pulley in the closet so that the buckets of dirt could be raised to the upper level. We girls would empty the bucket out of a back door, and this created a level platform behind the cabin for more parking space. The pulley system was set up in the closet so that he could continue working when it rained or snowed. He was resourceful and worked hard, never short on ingenuity, and I always admired those qualities about him.

Dad also built a shower out of one of the closets so

we could take showers inside rather than bathing in a tub in the backyard. Things were looking up! And no more outhouse either. (We had a special outhouse—a two-seater! My sister and I could go out together at night, and then my two brothers got their turn.)

I will always cherish those days when we went without all the modern facilities and conveniences. It was real family time, sitting by the fireside popping popcorn in the fireplace the old-fashioned way, talking about our daily experiences, and sharing our lives together. It's an important thing the families of today miss out on since iPhones have come to town!

There was one morning when my dad was coming home from the market and saw a young eagle in the street struggling with something. He stopped to check it out and found that the eagle had a bone caught in its throat. With the help of my two brothers, he got the eagle into the car and took it home. Dad put it on the workbench, cut the eagle's throat open, removed the bone, sewed him up, put him in a pen, and then nursed him back to health.

My family had just moved all their things from Pasadena to Big Bear, one of which was the bird aviary he had raised canaries in. Dad put the eagle in the aviary and he and Mom fed the eagle for about two months. At the end of that time, they felt he was strong enough to take care of himself. We all stood watching as Dad let him out of the aviary.

The eagle stumbled around a bit, flapped its wings for a while, and then took off. He circled around and around and then he was gone. The next season, one morning Dad looked up in the tree behind the cabin and saw his eagle. Dad had some fish in his freezer, so he threw it out on the driveway. The eagle swooped down, snatched it in his claws, and took it up into the tree to eat it. There is an old Indian tale that if you ever befriend an eagle, it will return every year. This eagle did return for many years and lots of stories were told and pictures taken of "Ted Ducey's eagle."

(Decades later, in my dad's later years, a woman named Lynn Montgomery bought Gold Mountain Manor in Big Bear and made it into a bed and breakfast. Because of the eagle story, she named one of the bedrooms the Ted Ducey Room. She was so helpful in keeping him busy in his final years; it helped him not to miss Mom so much. Lynn would pick him up, take him to the manor for breakfast with her guests, and he would tell them eagle stories. She would also take him along on their boat tours and Dad would point out the eagles' habitats. It helped her in her business and it helped me to keep him happy during those last years of his life.)

In my late teen years, I got very involved at school with singing in quartets, choirs, solos, and trios. Then I joined a group of forty gals that traveled to various places to sing for servicemen during the war. We were called the Nysaean singers.

One trip was a four-day bus journey to Blythe, California. We stayed right in the barracks, which was pretty interesting with their latrines and all. It was such an exciting time, singing for the boys who were fighting for our country, knowing how much it lifted their spirits out in those hotspots. Some of the songs we sang in those days included "Smoke Gets in Your Eyes," "When the Lights Go On Again," "As Time Goes By," and "God Bless America."

My first job in Big Bear was working for Safeway Stores. I was there for four years. I signed up for two post-graduate courses at the high school (Typing and Music) so I could ride on the school bus. My boss at Safeway would send someone to pick me up and take me to work the rest of the day and I would ride home on the bus. That was until I bought my first car, a Nash coupe. Everybody laughed at my car, but it ran and was paid for, and that's all I cared about.

When I would drive to work, there was a little man who worked at the restaurant across from the store where I worked. Once he knew I had a car, he would stand out on the road and thumb a ride. I picked him up and he would ride to work with me every day. Pretty soon he started bringing his dog along, a Pomeranian that I don't think ever had a bath! He carried the dog in its little cage, but it stank!

One night after work, it was snowing and we were on our way home and my car broke down. We were not far from a phone so I asked him if he would be nice enough to walk back to the phone and call my dad to come help. This man never paid gas money and I felt that making the walk in the snow was the least he could do in this situation, but he wouldn't do it! So I left my car and walked in the snow to call my dad, who came to help.

The next day, he was standing out for his regular ride and I picked him up as usual. But when I got on the straightaway I purposely "pulled a brodie" (put the brakes on and spun the car completely around), making two full circles before coming to a stop. We went on to work, but he never stood out thumbing a ride again. I had given him the ride of his life, I guess! (No more smelly dog either!)

Big Bear is in the San Bernardino Mountains of California. A checker at the Big Bear Safeway store would normally have to go "down the hill" to attend a three-month training program. However, because the boss was a friend of my dad, he let me train in Big Bear. I started as a "box boy" for a short time, then worked with other departments—produce, meat, dairy, and deli—so I would be familiar with everything in the store and its location.

Finally, I trained on the check register and learned how to work it. If we were to have a snowstorm and the electricity went off, we had to know how to hand-crank the register. I had a really good teacher, Bertha

Burton, who taught me how to make change, where to put the money, how to balance to the penny every night, and how to be pleasant to the customers if they were difficult (and we definitely had some of those).

I was young and caught on fast, ending up with the record for the fastest, most accurate cashier in the chain at that time. On my breaks and lunch hour, I would sit in the back room and crochet squares for a bedspread! The popcorn stitch, it was called. A neighbor taught me how and I enjoyed doing it. By the end of four years working there, I had completed the whole bedspread for my hope chest.

Those were good years for me. My boss and his wife had three children: two girls and a boy. They would invite me to go horseback riding with them, which I enjoyed very much. When the fruit was still good but unsellable, my boss let me take home the cherries and apples and I would make cobblers and bring them to work for lunch the next day. I enjoyed doing it, and of course they liked the goodies.

At the store, one fellow kept coming through my check stand every night at about 5:00 when he got off of work. He would come in to shop for his family and would flirt and joke with me. "What do you want me to buy for our dinner tonight?" he would ask, as if he were planning to go home and fix it and have it ready when I got home. I would go along with it to a point, all the time wondering where his wife was.

He finally brought her in, and then later, two of his sisters and his brother. They all decided I would be a perfect wife for their brother who had been in Iwo Jima in the Marines for forty-four months and would soon be coming home. They brought a picture of him to show me how handsome he was. I have to admit, I was infatuated with him before I even met him.

The young man, John, came home from Iwo Jima and we met and got acquainted. My boss invited us all to go horseback riding together with his family. We did, and I was charmed and enamored with John L. (His middle name was Lawrence and I always called him John L.) It was a full moon for our horseback ride, and I was singing the Indian love call in those mountains. Three months later, in September, we were married.

The following New Year's Eve, we went to a party with John L.'s family. Six of the wives at the party were going to have babies, and on the spur of the moment, we decided, "Let's make it seven." That's all the thought we put into it! Our reasoning was, "We're married, we have a good job, we're both twenty-two years old—why not?" I believe we became pregnant that very night, and nine months later, Clifford was born.

I got John L. a job at the grocery store, but my boss couldn't keep us both, so John L. took my place and I stepped down. It only took a month to find out that he didn't like to work indoors. He wanted to be out in the open, so we moved down the hill to the Hollywood area, where his mother and five sisters lived. We bought a little house in San Fernando Valley, I went to work at Ralphs Market, and John L. worked delivering propane.

We had some good times. There was boating, camping, and skiing with the boat clubs we belonged to. John L. had a friend from high school that we did boating to Catalina Island with. He had a really good boat and we entered some ski races, won trophies, and I loved the challenge.

In fact, one Saturday morning I skied all the way to Catalina and back—one hour and fifteen minutes there and, due to some rough waters, one hour and twenty minutes coming back. Sharks were just outside of the wake swimming right alongside me. My legs were like rubber afterward and I could not stand up or walk for about twenty minutes!

It was a time of building up—a career, a marriage, a family. But looking back, I was building rather hastily, and I wasn't much concerned with the foundation I was building on. The Bible says that a wise man builds his house upon rock and the foolish man builds upon sand. When the rains come, the house on the strong foundation will stand, but the house built upon sand will break down. Little did I know that the storms of trial and hardship were on their way...

6

A Time To Break Down

Buying a house meant new fences, landscaping, and furniture. That, with a baby coming, meant we were up to our eyeballs in debt!

Our baby was about nine months old the first time John L. was arrested. His arrest was for something as silly as taking a two-by-four off of a construction job. His brother-in-law got him off by saying it was in the street and that John L. was being a good guy and was taking it back to the building site.

Over the next thirteen years of our marriage, this arrest became a repeat performance—in and out of jail—but the offenses became worse. John L. couldn't hold a job very long and we depended on what I made to get by, in addition to borrowing against furniture or anything we had of value.

I kept up appearances and didn't let anyone know— not my friends, my neighbors, or my parents. Though divorce often crossed my mind, to me it was not an option as I was married in the Catholic Church, had taken an oath, and therefore was stuck!

That changed when I got sick, however. My back went out and I couldn't go up the stairs to my job. By this time, I had worked up to be head cashier of the Ralphs grocery store in the San Fernando Valley.

My dad said, "I'm taking you to my bone doctor to see what's wrong." I went. After examining me, the doctor said, "There is nothing wrong with your back, but what's wrong with your head? Want to tell me?"

In response, I dumped thirteen years of pent-up frustrations, unhappiness, and anger on him. My illness was psychosomatic, and so the doctor sent me to a counselor, who helped me make some decisions. She said, "You can continue to live with your husband and be sick the rest of your life, or you can divorce and move on with your life."

I went to two Jesuit priests and told them my story. They both said they would annul my marriage as I had plenty of reasons, which I won't go into. But when the priests told me they would annul my marriage, and that it would be as if I had never married in the first place, I began to think, "What would my son's name be? What would my son's identity be?"

In the end, I figured that if the priests agreed I had reason enough to annul the marriage, I was okay to get a divorce, and my son would at least be "legitimate." So I divorced John L. and moved on. As a divorced Catholic, I was resigned that I would never get married again.

The breakdown of my health, the breakdown of my marriage—all of it was extremely difficult. However, going through this hard time led to something good. It made me pick up my Bible and start reading it. I had bought a beautiful Bible when we were first married and I always had it on the mantel, and sometimes I would pull it down and look at the pictures, but we never read it.

I had always thought of God as being way out in the sky someplace—not near and personal. The divorce caused me to wake up a bit and I was determined to read my Bible from cover to cover. I found that there is a special blessing that one gets by reading all of it, and as I read through it, I could better understand how the Old Testament fit together with the New. It started making more sense, even though I didn't understand much of what I was reading.

Reading the Bible caused me to question so many things about my beliefs, especially that we don't have to go to a priest, the Pope, or Mary to talk to God. He is right where we are, and all we have to do is talk to Him, pray to Him, ask Him to forgive our sins and to help us with our needs and to give us wisdom.

Sometimes storms drive us to seek shelter. God allows trials in our life in order to direct us to Himself. My breakdown in health and the subsequent divorce were things that pushed me nearer to God. I was seeking answers, seeking truth, seeking God—and as the Lord says in Jeremiah 29:13, "If you look for me wholeheartedly, you will find me" (NLT).

7

A Time to Weep

Our friends Norm and Donna Carpenter felt so bad for me when I divorced John L. that they tried to set me up with friends of theirs. They would say, "Come on, Geneva, you aren't going to be a hermit the rest of your life!" They didn't understand that as a Catholic I was resigned that I wouldn't remarry.

I took my son and went to Hawaii to visit a school chum, Esther, who worked there in the Army PX (base store). She showed us around the island, and Cliff and I had a great time. It was 1959, the year Hawaii gained statehood. We went on Pan Am Airways; in those days you would fly in a prop plane, which took nine hours to get there.

Esther had a catamaran and we sailed all over Waikiki Bay. It was a great vacation after all I had been through. But like all great vacations, it came to an end, and I returned to California rested and recharged.

Coming home from Hawaii, I was happy to see that John L. had moved out. I didn't know where he was living or what he was doing.

My divorce was done, yet I still had the Catholic question in my head about it and I hadn't actually signed the final decree. It took me another year, and reading the Bible cover to cover, before I decided it was time to sign and make it final.

In the divorce, John L. was given visiting rights with our son. When and if he wanted to take Cliff for a weekend, John L. and I would meet for lunch and make the plans. I would insist that he follow our agreement because he had the tendency to play games.

After one of their visits around Christmastime, John L. brought Cliff back home. In addition, he brought something else through the door, quickly set it down, and walked right back out without a word. He didn't want to stick around because he knew I would be mad at what he had brought into my house. It was a cage with a monkey in it—a real, live, mess-making monkey. Now, I was working eight hours a day in addition to taking care of Cliff. The last thing in the world that I needed on my hands was a monkey!

As Cliff tried to take him out of his cage to show him off, the monkey was too fast for him and he started jumping all around the living room. The monkey ended up in the Christmas tree, but the glass in the angel hair on the tree must have hurt him. The monkey, tangled in the angel hair, was screaming in pain. I was screaming too, yelling for Cliff to get that monkey back into the cage. As Cliff got hold of him and put him in the cage, the monkey bit him.

I, of course, was extremely worried that Cliff could have been infected with rabies or some exotic disease. That worry only increased when the following day the monkey died!

I didn't know where John L. lived and didn't have a phone number for him. I had no way of contacting him and no way of knowing if the monkey was obtained legally or what its history was.

It was 3:45 p.m. on Friday and I called the health department, which closed at 4:00. Because it was too late in the day and they wouldn't open again until Monday, they instructed me to put the dead monkey in the freezer! "In the freezer?" I repeated. That threw me for a loop.

It was a stressful weekend waiting to see if Cliff would be all right, until I was able to take the frozen monkey in on Monday to have it tested. Fortunately, the monkey was not diseased and Cliff was fine, but the entire episode gives you a glimpse into John L.'s character and his disregard for me.

John L. had not been paying child support (a whopping fifteen dollars per month) and he owed me over seven hundred dollars back pay). I had decided to take him to court despite his promises to pay me.

One day when we met to discuss a visit with Cliff, John L. promised again that he would come up with the money, but he also added something interesting. He said, "What would you do if I held you up?" referring to robbing me at the store when I met the armored truck delivery (he knew that a 10:00 a.m. delivery was part of the daily routine). I told him, "I would push the button and you wouldn't get out of the store." He said, "You wouldn't do that to me, would you"? I answered with the same question: "You wouldn't do that to me, would you?" He just laughed.

After my lunch date with him, when I went back to work, my boss asked if John L. had paid me or if I still needed the coming Tuesday off to go to court. I told him yes, I still needed Tuesday off, and I also mentioned the remark he had made about holding me up. My boss said, "Geneva, we have to call security."

I sat down and cried. I was upset with myself for mentioning that remark to my boss, as I didn't think John L. really meant anything by it—John L. was just a prankster! The boss called the main office, and the security officer who came out as a result was a person I had gone to school with. I was mortified!

Tuesday came around, and I went to court to receive my seven hundred dollars, but John L. didn't show up. When I got back to work, my boss asked me if I had a picture at home of my ex-husband. (I lived just two blocks up the street.) He said, "We think John L. held up the Wilshire store."

As it turns out, it was him! He had stolen more than nine thousand dollars. During the robbery, John L. had left a paper on a desk with his fingerprints on it, so they had evidence it was him. He had held up my former boss and the woman who trained me. They recognized him as a customer but couldn't place where they had seen him before.

He had dressed in a suit and tie with a briefcase in his hand, gone in the back door of the store, and asked for the manager, who was in the back room. He told the manager he was there to make the final plans for the pancake breakfast they were putting on Saturday. The manager said he didn't know about it and would have to call the main office to confirm. John L. said, "That's fine. I'll go with you."

When they got into the office, the head cashier had all her money on the desk preparing to fill the registers for the day. The manager went to the phone to make the call, but John L. told him to put it down. John L. put the gun in the cashier's face and told her to fill his bag as fast as she could or there would be trouble.

Because he used a gun and because this was the ninth store they knew of, John L. was sentenced to five years to life. And, actually, I was relieved. No more problems from him, or so I thought. And yet, he got out in three years!

Needless to say, this event turned my whole life upside down. I was taken into the jail, as they were sure I was an accomplice when they found he had held up nine stores! He was buying new cars and furniture, had a nice apartment, and was living "high on the hog" while his son and I were struggling to make ends meet!

It turned out to be a protective blessing for me that I had told my boss about John L.'s comments to me. My boss was the one who stood up for me, convincing the authorities that I was a help in catching the thief. God had turned my "time to weep" into a blessing. He is always watching over those He loves and is able to take what we think is the worst thing and use it for our good.

8

A Time To Love

My second husband, Ted, was born in Los Angeles. His parents were from Holland and came through Ellis Island when they were young, around eighteen to twenty years old. Ted's dad came over to America with Ted's uncle, and they both got jobs in Los Angeles. The ladies came over shortly after and they soon married.

Ted had two sisters and one brother. Just like I lost my sister early on, Ted lost his brother, who drowned in Lake Tahoe.

Ted had a pretty normal life; he worked with his dad and learned a lot about business as his dad ran the Natick Hotel in downtown Los Angeles, which kept them busy. Ted's dad taught him the business part of running the hotel, how to get along with customers, how to make beds, collect money, make deposits, balance the money at the end of the day, and how to get rid of the rats in the basement. (Yes, rats!)

Ted went to Dorsey High School and then was drafted into the army. He spent most of his time in Korea as a radio technician. It was cold over there and not too comfortable. He longed to return home.

Around 1952 he came home and within the year, he married his longtime girlfriend, Joanne. They started a rug cleaning business out of their house and dedicated it to the Lord. It grew and things were going along well. They enjoyed boating and spent a lot of time at the marine stadium waterskiing.

About three years later, in 1955, their son Chuck was born. Before even leaving the hospital, Joanne noticed lumps under her arms. The birth had triggered Hodgkin's disease, so the next two and a half years were brutal for them. Willing to try any and every cure they could find, they heard of a "grape cure" at a facility in Tecate, Mexico. So Ted bought a little trailer for her and Chuck, and he took them to Mexico. Ted drove back and forth on the weekends to be with Joanne and Chuck, but they saw no progress. It became clear that it was time for her to go to UCLA Hospital, where she passed away at twenty-seven years old.

It was a very traumatic time for Ted. He was going through that hardship about the same time I had my problems.

Ted's sister Peggy had two children, Candice and Duffy, and she offered to take Chuck in to help Ted until he figured out his life and to give Chuck a more normal home environment.

Ted worked all day, went to Peggy's for dinner, tucked Chuck into bed, and went home to his ailing father, whose heart was failing. It was a lot to cope with. When I came into the picture, I didn't know any of this.

I first met Ted through Norm. You see, my ex-husband and I had a boat that we owed money on, so John L. took the boat into Norm's lot to sell. In the meantime, Ted had a boat that had slid off his trailer and he had brought it in to Norm's for repair. When our boat came into the shop, Norm called Ted to come look at ours to see if he'd want to buy our boat instead of fixing his.

Ted asked John L. why he was selling the boat, and John L. told him that his wife had kicked him out and in fact, he was looking for a place to live. Ted mentioned that he had a three-bedroom apartment and one of the guys had recently moved out. He invited John L. to take his place. Ted ended up buying the boat and John L. ended up moving in with Ted. Before long, Ted learned John L.'s true colors and since John L. wasn't paying rent, they kicked him out.

I didn't know about any of this; nor did I have the faintest notion that this man, Ted, would end up being my husband three years later!

Norm, not knowing that John L. had moved in with

Ted, asked Ted to double date with me. (I had been awarded dinner and dancing at the Moulin Rouge for being Cashier of the Month at the grocery store, and I really wanted to go, but didn't have a date to dance with.) Ted, who didn't realize that I was already divorced, told Norm no, and said that I should go with my husband.

It ended up being six of us that evening, Norm and Donna, Ted and a lady friend, my ex-husband, and me. Of course, John L. ignored me, would not pin the orchid on me given by the grocery store, and really played up to Ted's girlfriend. This opened up Ted's eyes to where I stood with John L. I still had a good time that night, and it was nice to get out in the world again!

I saw Ted many more times after that first "date." And it was like a Cinderella courtship. He swept me off my feet. He had his own airplane, would fly out to Van Nuys Airport, pick me up, and fly me to Catalina for a buffalo burger! Then he'd fly me back to work. I had a great boss who would give me a longer lunch hour as long as all my work got done.

Since we were both into waterskiing, Ted and I did a lot of that on weekends. Cliff and I used to ride up to Pine Flat Lake, California, with Peggy and her kids. Ted and Jeff (Peggy's husband) would fly. We would set up a tent for Cliff and me, and Ted and his family rented a motel. Ted's friends all joined us in their trailers and parked near our tent. It was like one big happy family.

I taught most of them how to ski, Jeff cooked the breakfast outdoors, which always smelled so good, and they were fun times.

Ted would pick up Cliff and me in the Valley, then head for Millerton Lake, California, for summer weekends. He had a jeep chained to a tree there, so he parked the plane and we jumped into the jeep and headed for the campground to meet Peggy, Jeff, and their family. We always had six or eight kids along in the jeep as Ted was a family man, and we all got along great. In town we would go to a dance or dinner with some of the friends he had made while married to Joanne.

It was a three-year courtship ending in a wedding in his sister's home. The same pastor who married Ted and Joanne also married us. We went off to Hawaii for our honeymoon—Oahu, Kauai, and the Big Island— and it was wonderful.

God has given me such a gift in Ted. He is honest, loving, and compassionate. He makes me laugh and always has ideas for fun adventures. He's full of life and he energizes me. He is a good father, stepfather, and grandfather. He's tidy and helpful. Every gift and even the greeting cards he picks out for me are thoughtful and given with such love and sincerity. We've been married for fifty-seven years now and I love our life together. I am grateful the Lord brought him into my life.

A Time to Sew

Blending two families is a bit like sewing together two pieces of fabric. Things don't always line up perfectly, and sometimes you have to go back and undo the messy parts, but in the end you find a way to work it all out and move on to the next thing.

Ted's son, Chuck, was four when I first met Ted and he was seven when we married. My son, Clifford, was fourteen when we married. So there was a difference of about seven years between them.

Coming from families where they were both "number one" in terms of our attention and affection, Cliff and Chuck both suddenly became number three once we got married—or at least, it sometimes felt that way. It was a big change.

At first Cliff really wanted his own dad because his dad was funny and did lots of fun things. You see, when all of the terrible things with my first husband were happening, I chose not to tell Cliff most of the details, as he was only eleven years old at the time. He had no idea what was going on and I felt it was better at the time to keep him in the dark about John L.'s true nature.

Sometimes I think in a panic we want to overprotect our kids instead of being open with them about what's going on. It wasn't until my son was about thirty that he wanted to know the reasons why we divorced.

Cliff loved his dad and as he saw it, I was wrong in taking his dad away from him. So when I finally started dating another man, there was rejection on Cliff's part. He didn't want a new father; he wanted his fun dad. He resisted the idea of a new family, at least at first.

Chuck, on the other hand, was looking forward to spending more time with his dad and moving into a new house. But it was a little difficult for him as well because Ted's sister Peggy had become such a big part of his life, acting in many ways as an interim mother after Ted's first wife passed away.

I really didn't put it together that he was living with her as his mom, so down the line there was some tension between Peggy and me concerning how Chuck should be raised, but Chuck was able to transition fairly well. One day, he came home from a visit to Peggy's and said, "I'm confused. I don't know. I don't want to call Peggy 'Mom' anymore. What can I call her?" I told him, "Well, why don't you just ask her what would make her happy and see if she wants you to call her Peggy, or what." She told him, "Just call me Peggy," so that's what he did from then on and he called me Mom. So he was comfortable with the change.

Overall, the boys got along pretty well. Of course, every once in a while, you'd hear the usual things from the backseat of the car—"You're sitting on my side" or "Put your foot over on your side"—and they'd argue. Sometimes Cliff would put a towel over his head and pout when he didn't like what was going on.

At first, Ted and I may have had to fight the tendency to take sides. I felt that Ted babied his "baby" a bit too much and didn't want to "put an apron" on his kid, if you will, and get him to work. Ted, on the other hand, felt that since Cliff was so much older, he should set the example and do most of the heavy lifting when it came to chores, which in my thinking let Chuck off the hook too much.

Things like this were just issues, discussions—never big arguments. We could usually sit down, talk about it, and then the boys would understand the final outcome: You're taking the trash out and he's mowing the lawn, etc. Overall, I think we did pretty much like normal families do. There are always going to be arguments and fusses.

Cliff was fourteen when Ted and I married, but he went into the service just short of eighteen. So from then on it was just Chuck at home. Between school, track running, Cub Scouts, and his other interests, we kept busy and there were a lot of fun times in those days.

Sewing our two families together brought about a good result, and it reminds me that as God adopts each of us into His family, He is constantly adding new squares onto the patchwork quilt of His kingdom—which makes it more and more beautiful and diverse. I want to be a part of that important work He is doing of bringing people into His family!

10

A Time to Plant

I retired from Ralphs Grocery thinking I was going to be a stay-at-home mom. Ted said, "Let's stop by the shop and see how things are going." Surprise! He had just won the bid to clean the rugs and body pads for 625 Los Angeles city schools! The rugs and pads had to be picked up, cleaned, and delivered back within the next three months. There went my retirement!

We both dove right in on Monday morning to get ready for something I had no idea about! I was used to office work, as I had been the head cashier and in charge of seven registers—but rugs? I didn't have a clue. I did learn fast and we got the job done.

Once I learned the lingo of rug cleaning as well as the prices and procedures, it was fun to go to work. Sometimes there would be only one job in the book for the day, but I would fill it up so we had a full day. Ted would run the trucks, men, and chemical solutions in the back of the shop, and I would run the office, schedule the jobs, count the money, and take care of the phones and banking.

For me, things were going too slowly on the Los Angeles school project, so I suggested I take a route of twenty-five schools per day, go ahead of our truck, and have the school custodian put the rugs out on the curb. That way, all we had to do was verify the count, write up the order, load the rugs onto the truck, and head for the next school. It saved so much time and money not having three men sitting around while each school tracked down their custodian.

Our office girl's mother lived in the Valley so two nights a week, after picking up the orders, we'd go to her house, where her mom would have dinner for us. There, I would write up the orders, she would type them, and we'd prepare the statements. Being ready with the statements when we delivered the rugs back meant that we'd get paid faster. We had a really good system and it went smoothly. We also made sure to deliver the rugs back on time.

Our business started growing. One day while Ted was out making estimates, he noticed a building with chains on the doors. He investigated and found it was in foreclosure, so we bought it.

We soon moved to the new location and we had more business than we could handle! Within the next year, we had eleven trucks and twenty employees!

Those early days of work in the rug business were

kind of like planting a garden. We worked hard and were diligent. Just as God sends rain in a garden, He showered blessings on us, and eventually we would reap the fruits of our labor.

11

A Time to Dance

One time, Ted and I attended a convention in Hong Kong. Part of the convention's itinerary included a dinner dance.

We were on the top floor of a high building with sixteen other rug cleaners, and the music was playing. Ted and I don't always dance well together; that's just how it is. We haven't gone to a lot of dances in our life, but that particular night when Ted and I got up to dance, for some reason we really clicked. Our colleagues at the convention were all older, and none of them got up to dance, so all eyes were on us.

Something about the music they were playing allowed us to dance in tandem. He would swing me around and we would swing back together. We'd be side by side going backwards and forwards and all of our movements were flowing and graceful that night. It was just so nice.

Both of us were surprised, when we went back to the

table, how many compliments we got, and we were a bit surprised ourselves at how well we had danced, and that made us both feel good.

On that same trip, we visited Japan and got out into one of the cities to see what life was like there. We went to the marketplace and saw many interesting things for sale, such as frogs and snakes for eating. After visiting the marketplace and seeing lots of interesting things for sale, we noticed some fabric floating in the river. Curious, we followed the fabric up the river to find out where it started. We discovered the source to be a factory that dyed silk, and after dying it they would let the river wash out the excess dye and it would give the fabric a unique look and coloring.

These are just sweet and simple memories of a good and happy trip, and I praise God that He allows such times in our lives. There are hard times and there are easy times, good times and bad times—and through it all God remains the same loving and caring Father. Psalm 136 says that we should "give thanks to the Lord, for He is good! For His mercy endures forever."

A Time to Keep

Ted and I had moved into our house in Ladera Heights. Ted brought all of his and Joanne's belongings, including their books, which I placed on shelves in the den.

While having dinner, sometimes we four (Ted, Cliff, Chuck, and I) would try to remember the Ten Commandments but could only come up with seven or eight. One night I went to our den and grabbed the first Bible I saw, which turned out to be Joanne's. When I opened it, a pink envelope fell out. I handed it to Ted, asking, "Have you seen this?" He got up from the table and went to the other room to read it. It had been stored in that Bible, unread, for the four years since Joanne's death. It said:

> *To my husband at my death,*
>
> *My darling, the time we've been dreading is finally at hand, our goodbye time. It's the hardest thing I've ever had to say.*

But one day (and the signs show it will be soon), we will say hello again and be reunited with my son. Take good care of him, feed him, nourish his little body properly so the pangs of disease will never touch him. Make sure Peggy, or whoever takes him, will get my books and literature. Raise him to know God and love him. Give him an education so he at least has a complete knowledge of the Bible.

As I lie here dying, I know it is what he would wish if he were dying. I'll always love you darling, even through eternity, into which I'm about to step. Have a good life, my Dear. Find him a good mother and yourself a good wife."

Love, Joanne

Ted later showed me the letter, and that presented me with a new challenge from Chuck's mom to raise him as she would want. It was very sobering. I resolved to keep Joanne's wishes as best as I could, and this resolution also helped to draw me closer to the Lord.

13

A Time To Laugh

We worked hard for six years without a vacation, other than long weekends, so it was time for a rest. We took a cruise to Hawaii with our son Chuck. Cliff was in Vietnam by then.

Ted and Chuck did a lot of scuba diving to see coral and fish and they had a great time together. I would be in a little rowboat above them. If they drifted too far, they could get into the dinghy with me and we could all ride back to our boat. The boys brought up nice coral; we would dry them out and bleach them to remove the odor and make them pure white.

When we traveled, we would usually wash our clothes on the last night of the trip so that they would arrive home clean, without saltwater in them. That's what we did for this trip as well. On the night before our flight home, I washed everything and hung it out to dry in the nice evening breeze. Of all things, it decided to rain, so we brought them in and tried to dry them out, but there wasn't enough time. So after we packed the coral, the leftover food, and whatever else, we put the wet clothes on top, leaving the box open as we had to go through customs.

The manager of the complex we were staying in offered to take us to the airport on his way to church. He arrived, we packed our things into the car, and we all headed to the airport. He pulled up right in front of the conveyer belts where everyone was standing in line. My husband got out of the car, grabbed the big box with the wet clothes, and the bottom fell out because the cardboard had become damp! Everything went flying.

A bottle of ketchup broke, the coconuts rolled through the ketchup, and the man who drove us leaned over to pick up some items and his tie dipped into the ketchup (remember he was on his way to church). The white coral was now red. My husband was so embarrassed, he started throwing things in the trash. I was digging them out of the trash as my son wanted to keep the things they had dived for.

Everyone in line was laughing their heads off. It was like a scene from *I Love Lucy*.

The airport workers brought us new boxes, saying, "Forget inspection. Just wrap it up!" We finally got organized, the driver left, we checked in for our flight, and we got on the plane, ready for home. Not speaking to each other now, after a five-hour flight, we arrived in California, the boxes were on the conveyer belt, and as we picked one of them up, the same thing happened!

It didn't feel very funny at the time, but looking back on it, I can't help but laugh. The Bible says, "The cheerful heart has a continual feast" (Proverbs 15:15 NIV). Over the years, God has given me many reasons to laugh and so much joy. I'm grateful to Him for those blessings and for the gift of laughter.

14

A Time To Throw Away

We sold our airplane after many years of enjoying it. We had taken many trips to Cabo San Lucas, bringing another couple with us as we were into playing tennis. We had great food, the Mariachis played for us every night, and those were nice getaway weekends. We went as far as Tampico on one trip and when we got into motorhoming, we went to the tip of Baja with other friends who had motorhomes. We all camped out with bonfires and told tales to each other.

Our motorhome experiences were a learning process, so we found it helpful to join a motorhome club. We bought a lot in an RV park in Cathedral City to go there for long weekends. We would leave the RV on the lot during weekends or even spend a couple of weeks at a time there in the desert. We also bought a lot on a river in Oregon along with the same group from Cathedral City and when it turned hot, we would all go to Oregon for salmon fishing together. Those were fun times where we would go crabbing, come back to camp, and have cooked crab along the riverside. It was a beautiful spot.

One of our motorhome club members was named Glen Patch and he was quite wealthy, but he was also very generous and he loved people. He would organize extravagant parties and trips that were a lot of fun to attend. He would charge a reasonable fee to attend, and the fee would be used to support a good cause or something that would benefit the local community.

I remember that he had bought an old town from back east, removed the facades from the buildings there, and then shipped them to Montana, where he placed them on new buildings that he had constructed. It was basically a brand-new town that was made to look like an old country town. He invited the entire RV club (about fifty motorhomes) to come and enjoy it. Artists and sculptors and chefs were all on hand to entertain and treat us.

That was just one of many gala events that he put on, and we enjoyed ourselves very much on all of the luxurious trips that Glen made available to our motorhome club.

When you hang around in clubs and there is drinking at night, everyone joins in. We found that as time went on, some of the group would start drinking at 10:00 in the morning with a Bloody Mary, then at noon it was vodka and orange juice, and by 5:00 p.m., they were pretty stoned.

When we became born again, that life was no longer a good option for us.

At one point, we were having custom work done on our motorhome. Part of the agreement was that at the end of the conversion, they could display the motorhome as a show coach for their company. So it was no surprise that when we went to check on the work being done, we heard a knock on the RV door and it was the manager of the company bringing a couple who wanted to see inside.

I welcomed them in and, friendly as could be, I showed them the two TVs, the wine cabinet with the glass door engraved with grapes, etc. There was a liquor bottle on the kitchen counter, and other booze in storage. The couple looked over the RV, said thank you, and left. The couple's driver, whose name was Judd, came over and asked if I knew who they were. I said, "No, should I?"

He said, "You will," and left.

The time came when the coach was completed and it was time to go to Arizona to display it. We had it all set up with liquor in the bottles, wine in the wine cabinet, four wine glasses on the table, etc. Another knock on the door and the manager had the same couple to look at the finished coach. They had an RV of their own and planned on upgrading. They looked it all over, said it was very nice, and again they left.

Judd came again to the door and asked, "Do you know who they are yet?"

"No, please tell us," we said.

He told us, "Wait, I will be right back." He came back and handed me a book titled *The Cross and the Switchblade* by David Wilkerson, evangelist and founder of the addiction recovery ministry Teen Challenge. That couple was Mr. and Mrs. David Wilkerson.

After the showing was over, we headed to Palm Springs, where we would spend the summer. I started to read the book and couldn't put it down. I had finished it by the time we arrived in Palm Springs. While reading the local paper, I read an advertisement that said David Wilkerson was coming to town and would be speaking Friday, Saturday, and Sunday of the following week. I said to Ted, "I want to go hear him, but we are not drinking as I don't want alcohol on my breath!"

We went to the event and sat right down in the front row so we could see and hear well. David came out on the stage and up to the podium. He started speaking and greeted everyone. Shortly after that, funny noises were coming out from the crowd—many people started speaking in tongues! My husband and I looked at each other, knowing we were in the wrong place, but we couldn't leave because we were in the front seats! At the first break, David came down off the stage and walked right up to me to say hello. He welcomed us and I said, "We were the couple with the motorhome." He said, "Yes, I know, and you are not here by mistake; you have been anointed by the Lord!"

We weren't sure what he meant but we stayed and came back Saturday and Sunday. Over time, we became good friends with David. I got on his mailing list and we became donors to his ministry. That was 1984 and we are still very involved with his ministry today.

I think that experience was the first step toward me throwing away the bottle, so to speak.

The actual day that I gave up hard liquor was when I felt a desire to share the *Jesus* film project with many people and I went to Pastor Chuck Smith to ask for his help in backing the project.

I knew that Pastor Chuck was absolutely against any kind of drinking because his dad was an alcoholic. So it came to me in the night that I couldn't go to him with this request if I were drinking, and I prayed, "Lord, take that desire away from me." And He did.

I consider that one of the many miracles in my life. I wasn't an alcoholic, but I enjoyed drinking with everybody else. So for the Lord to take the desire away completely and permanently was a blessing.

Ted and I still drink wine on occasion. The doctor

says it's good for the tummy. I'm sure that if I had continued drinking hard liquor, I probably would have ended up like many of our friends who would start drinking earlier and earlier in the day, and my life would have been shorter than it has been. As it was, I was up to two drinks a night and maybe even cheating on three, so to give it up completely was something extraordinary.

So, while I don't want to give the impression that drinking alcohol is a sin, I am grateful that the Lord was able to help me throw away that habit.

15

A Time to Cast Away Stones

It was the end of summer in 1974, and Ted and I had been married for about twelve years. We had moved from Ladera Heights to Newport Beach. My parents were still living in Big Bear and as they aged, the winters were getting to be too much for them. They had a house trailer, so we kids decided to take the trailer down to the Colorado River, set it up for them, surprise them for their anniversary, and take them down for Labor Day weekend. They loved to fish and always enjoyed the river.

We planned a weekend when all of us would go down and hook things up so that my parents could just move in. My brother Ted and his wife, along with two of their six children, went down early to hook up the water and the toilet. We were to go Friday after work, and my other brother Jerry was to meet us there. Both Jerry and I had something come up so we couldn't make it on Friday after all. We planned to go Saturday morning.

The place where the trailer was set up was called Nelson's Landing, just below the town of Nelson. There was an alarm system in place that when it started raining in Nelson, they would warn people at the landing that flash flooding might occur.

That's what happened on this weekend. Those who were already there were warned that there would be flash floods. They were told to pull up their chairs and watch it, as it was fun to watch the water go so fast!

My family knew enough about flash flooding to know you should get to high ground. My brother was working on my folks' trailer; his wife and two kids were in the trailer next door. His twelve-year-old son went to tell him that there was going to be a flood. Ted told his wife he was going down to talk to the ranger to see how bad it was.

As he turned around and went out the door, the flood of mud, boulders, and debris suddenly came rolling down the ramp where the boats are launched, and straight toward all the trailers. He jumped on the roof of his car as it washed away down the ramp. Ted was hanging on for dear life. A man was in the water calling for help, so my brother leaned over to pull him onto the car with him. But the car rolled over and away they both went into the flood. Ted was never seen again!

Nine people were killed that day. Some were washed as far as two miles up the river. When we arrived, they had stopped the river upstream, so it was no longer flowing into Nelson's Landing. The whole area looked like a lake you could walk on, filled with mud and debris—broken skis, ice chests, destroyed boats, and trailers that were twisted and broken to bits. How could anyone be found alive in all of that?

There were eight of us in our family who arrived. Ted's wife and two children were taken to the hospital with others. The eight of us lined up in a row and started turning things over with the hope Ted might be under an upside-down boat, trapped in a bubble of air somewhere. People were popping up all over, some with their clothes stripped off by the flood.

My brother Jerry was in the construction business, so he went to Yucca to get two trucks and a steam shovel to start digging. The government was sending a large piece of equipment, but it wouldn't arrive till the next day. The flood had left at least twelve feet of mud and rocks on the ramp. If ever there was "a time to cast away stones" this was it.

When Jerry came back with the steam shovel, we all lined up on the bank to watch as he cleared the mud from the ramp. With each shovel load, we looked to see if Ted was there. It was heart-wrenching. On one hand, we wanted him found, but on the other hand, we hoped he wouldn't be there—that somehow he was on the other side of the river, safe.

My brother Ted had been the head coach at

Claremont McKenna College. He was in good shape, ran a swim school, and wasn't one to panic. Because of that, we were sure he must have survived somehow. But they went up and down the river with a search helicopter to no avail. We never found my brother.

How could this be? Such a great guy, always helping others, a wife and six kids. *God, what are you doing?* I was so mad at God!

As time went on, I began to see the blessings that came out of this horrible experience. A year later, the school built a new gymnasium and named it after him: the Ducey Gym. At the dedication, one young student got up to say he had been on alcohol and Ted tried to get him to stop. He announced he had not had a drink since my brother died.

A few years later, while reading the *Big Bear Grizzly* paper, I saw a picture of a person I recognized. I read the article and the man in it told of his dad's best friend being killed in a flash flood. At the time, this fellow was not on the right track; he was going downhill. But the death of my brother was a wake-up call to him. He made a commitment to himself to change and the article was announcing him as the senior pastor at Calvary Chapel Big Bear.

So you see, things can be brutal, and we wonder why, but we must always look for the blessings that can come out of tragedy, and we know that God is in charge and has a plan.

16

A Time to Embrace

Being raised a Catholic, I always assumed I was right with Jesus, yet I thought He was distant. I never knew you really could talk to Him and know Him.

It wasn't until around age sixty that Ted and I ended up attending church at South Coast Community Church, led by Pastor Tim Timmons. Pastor Tim was a good instructor and a good speaker. I connected with his teaching. It was then, in 1984, that Ted and I accepted the Lord into our lives.

At first, I thought I was going to have a special feeling, but I didn't, so I still didn't fully understand that I could have an intimate relationship with the Lord. It took another good year before it really hit my breastplate and, from that point forward, I just knew what direction I was going. There was no question in my mind.

I fully embraced the Lord and His plan for me. Since that time, I've been working for Him. I may have started late, but God promises that He will make up for lost time, which makes me so happy, and He certainly has blessed the years since I turned my life over to Him.

As I started to walk more closely with the Lord and listen to His voice, different incidents in my life would confirm to me that I was on the right track with Him. You might just consider them coincidental, but for me they were reminders that God is with me and that I am important to Him.

For instance, a few years later when we were attending Calvary Chapel Costa Mesa, there was a time one Sunday when we were headed to church as usual and I noticed a man standing in the street. He looked to me like he was in need. I said to Ted, "Let's turn around and see if he needs help or a ride." We did turn around and when he spoke, it was in broken English. He said "Church, church, Pastor Chuck Smith?" We finally figured he wanted a ride. He was from out of town and trying to find the church where Chuck Smith was the pastor, and that just happened to be exactly where we were going! So he hopped in and went with us. It turns out he was to help Pastor Chuck translate some of his books and writings into a foreign language.

Another time, I was helping a friend of mine, Marta Hemphill, to pare down her things in preparation for a move. She had many antiques and unique objects.

In thanks for my help, she gave me a very beautiful lamp that I had admired and that matched the colors in my home. It turns out this lamp had originally belonged to Henrietta Mears, who was a godly woman that taught Sunday school and impacted many prominent Christian leaders, including Billy Graham.

Years later, when I had become friends with Bill and Vonette Bright, the founders of Campus Crusade for Christ, Vonette recognized the lamp because she and Bill had lived in and taught out of Henrietta Mears' house for ten years. Vonette requested that when I die, I leave the lamp to her son so that it can remain with someone who appreciates its history, and I fully intend to do so.

Again, these "coincidences" may not be significant to you, but each one confirms that God is both interested in and at work in everything that goes on in my life.

17

A Time to Kill

After we gave our lives over to the Lord, I wanted to be baptized. Ted was gone on a project that we had going in Lake Tahoe, and South Coast Community Church was going to have a baptism that next weekend. So I called Ted and told him I wanted to get baptized because I was ready for that step. I had been baptized as a baby in the Catholic Church, but I wanted to make a public stand for my faith now that I had given my life to Him.

"Well, don't you want to wait until I come home and get baptized together?" Ted asked. I had assumed he didn't want to be baptized because he had already been baptized when he was married to Joanne. But Ted also wanted to make an outward demonstration of his faith in Jesus now that he was born again.

"If you want to get baptized together, I'll certainly wait. Yes, I would like to be baptized together," I told Ted. So when he came home from the project, he and I were baptized together at South Coast.

In Colossians, the apostle Paul tells us to "put to death whatever belongs to your earthly nature" and in Romans, he speaks of our old nature being crucified with Christ.

Baptism is a symbol of our putting to death and burying our sinful lives and then rising again in the newness of God's Holy Spirit. Going under the water represents putting away our sinful ways, and coming back up out of the water is a picture of being resurrected to a new life in Christ.

There is "a time to kill" in the life of every believer—a time to kill our sinful habits and routines, our old selves, and to follow Christ as new creations.

18

A Time to Speak

After I came to the Lord and was really on fire, spiritually speaking, I was listening to Christian radio and heard an advertisement for a 365-day Bible, and I felt I just needed to get one. So I ordered a copy and I read it from cover to cover.

I liked this version of the Bible so well that I ordered a case of them and started giving them out to our motorhome group. God gave me a boldness to talk to them about spiritual things, and he continues to give me boldness in sharing my faith even today.

In fact, just days ago, I had a unique experience. Ted and I pulled up to a shop where he needed to purchase some socks. Ted went into the store and I remained in the car. As I was sitting in the car, the lady in the vehicle next to me started honking her horn. I looked over at her and she was gasping. I opened the door and I said, "Are you all right?" She shook her head no and so I got out of the car (slowly, of course. I'm in my nineties!) to see how I could help.

I opened her door and I said, "What can I do for you? Do you want me to call 9-1-1?" She shook her head no, but she was still gasping and gasping. I asked her, "Do you know the Lord? Let's call on the Lord." She shook her head no and I said, "We're going to call on the Lord right now and ask Him to help you calm down." Then I prayed for her.

After she calmed down and got some air, she said, "I have these seizures every once in a while," and I had a little chance to talk to her. I asked, "What do you have against the Lord?" and she said, "Well, where was He when three men raped me when I was twelve years old?" Oh, what a terrible burden this woman had been carrying around for so many years!

I did my best to explain that God was not the cause of such a thing, that He wasn't absent, and that Satan is the true enemy who wants to harm us. God allows bad things to happen because He is preparing us to use us for some good purpose. I told her not to blame God, but to blame Satan instead.

I talked to her a little bit more and then I said, "I want you to remember this incident and I want you to think on what I said, because He's got you. He's watching you and you need Him when you have these seizures."

She said, "You are so sweet. Thank you for coming to my rescue." She had called her son, who was now on the way, so I said, "Well, I've done all I can do right now, but I want you to think about it."

These incidents can come up at any moment and we have to be ready for them. They are opportunities to point people to Jesus and get them thinking about the Lord.

I don't want to be bashful in telling others about Him.

A Time to Keep Silence

I mentioned before that there came a time when there was a rift between me and Peggy, Ted's sister. At first, Peggy and I were very, very good friends. She took me out to help me pick out my wedding dress and my wedding ring. There was waterskiing together and camping together and many visits to their house, so it was a good relationship as far as I knew. After Ted's wife had died, their son, Chuck, went to live with Peggy and she in many ways filled that motherly role in Chuck's life until Ted married me.

We didn't find out until much later how hard it was for Peggy to give up Chuck to me, and her thoughts about how Chuck should be raised were different than ours, especially when it came to religion.

One Thanksgiving, Ted asked Peggy why she thought their folks never went to church and why their family never talked about the Lord when they were growing up. Peggy got defensive and said that they certainly did go to church and they certainly did talk about the Lord. But when pressed to name a time they all went to church together, she couldn't. They argued and that caused a six-month period of no talking.

Ted and I tried to smooth it over and so did the boys, but to no avail. The following week, I wrote her a letter to ask forgiveness for hurting her feelings and I tried to explain it in a different way, but it didn't work.

I think in Peggy's mind, I was to blame for all of the arguing and the conflict in the family, and the focus of her issues centered around me. So later on, she wrote a birthday letter to Ted, mentioning that Peggy would call Ted and that she'd like to get together with "just the boys"—in other words, Chuck and Ted, no Geneva.

Ted called Peggy and asked, "Why not Geneva? We've never gone without Geneva." And she said, "Well, I just want to get together with the boys." His answer was, "I don't want to go behind Geneva's back, so that's not going to work for me." I was really glad he stood up for me.

About six months later, Peggy's daughter Candice called us up and said, "Can't we put this together? My mom wants to see her brother." I told her, "The door is always open. We've tried. I've written a letter. Ted has tried."

Candice replied, "Okay. Henry and I will come down and monitor a meeting if you'll come to Peggy's house and meet with her." (Henry is Candice's husband.) We said we would be glad to, we asked that it be around 1:00 in the afternoon on a certain date, and stipulated that there was to be no drinking before the meeting. Candice said she would make sure that happened.

The night before, I was praying, "What do You want us to do, Lord? How do You want this meeting to go?" and into my mind came the letter that Joanne wrote to Ted before she died. You'll recall that the letter requested Chuck be raised in the ways of the Lord, so it was something that Peggy might be able to understand concerning why God and going to church were so important to our family.

I got Joanne's letter out, reread it, and felt that it was the answer to what we should say to Peggy. She had never seen or known about that letter.

So the next morning, when Ted got up, before we went to Peggy's house, I told him about the letter coming to mind as I prayed and said, "I want you to reread Joanne's letter and then ask yourself if it is something you would want to use with Peggy today." He read it and he had the same feeling that I had. He told me, "Put it in your purse and if I want it, you'll have it available."

We got to the meeting and Peggy talked first. She attacked with all vengeance for about ten minutes. Then Candice, acting as a moderator, said, "Mom, now it's Ted's turn and he has as much right to attack you as you just attacked him. Are you ready for that?" She said, "Well, he can say whatever he wants."

Instead of attacking, Ted lovingly opened with, "Peggy, I want to thank you for everything you've done for me, and I want to apologize for anything that I've ever said or done to hurt you." (I get emotional just thinking about it.) He was very soft and kind.

Then he turned to me and he said, "Geneva, would you read the letter that Joanne wrote?" None of them had heard this letter, so I got it out of my purse and I started reading it, and of course it was hard not to be emotional as I read it, especially when you're with the family that experienced her young death, and I was just an "outsider," so to speak.

After reading the letter, the room was very heavy with emotion and Candice said, "I think we need to take a break right now." So Ted turned to Peggy and said, "Let's go in the kitchen a minute." In the kitchen Ted asked Peggy, "Do you have a little wash bin and some water and a towel?" And she said, "Well, what is this all about?" but she provided what he asked for.

Ted told her, "Let's go in the other room, and sit back down again." Starting with Candice's husband Henry, then moving to Candice and then Peggy, Ted asked each of them to take off their shoes and socks, and then proceeded to wash their feet.

When he got to Peggy, she said, "You're not going to wash my feet." And he said, "Yes, I am. Take off your shoes and your socks." She did, and he washed her feet.

By this time everybody was crying and it was so emotional. It was a powerful act of humility, and it completely ended the argument.

In the book of Exodus, as the children of Israel are being pursued by Pharaoh's army, they are fearful. Moses tells them, "Fear not, stand firm, and see the salvation of the Lord, which he will work for you today ... The Lord will fight for you, and you have only to be silent" (14:13–14 ESV).

The Lord fought for me that day, working through Ted, through Joanne's letter, and through the powerful example of Jesus washing the feet of His disciples. I just needed to be silent.

Later down the line, Peggy developed Lou Gehrig's disease (ALS) and it's a very painful way to die. The day before she died, Candice called us and told us, "If you want to say goodbye to Mom, now is the time." So we went to Santa Barbara and arrived to find Peggy thrashing in the bed with pain. Everybody took a moment to go to her side and talk to her, doing the best they could to comfort her. When it was my turn, she took my hand and told me, "Geneva, I want you to forgive me for everything I've done."

"I forgave you a long time ago," I replied, "It's all history."

20

A Time To Refrain From Embracing

As you get older, you find that there are times when you have to let go of dear friends.

I mentioned before that Norm and his wife, Donna, were very good friends of ours. Norm had been a friend even during my first marriage and he introduced me to Ted, so we had a very close relationship all through the years. Their son Doug and our son Chuck were three weeks apart in age; they had a band together and you would often find the boys practicing in our living room after school. Those were fun years. I became a den mother when Chuck was in the Cub Scouts. We held the meetings at our house, so it seemed like the house always had lots of boys around.

One year, they were into building their own slot car. Chuck did a great job on his and he won first prize for it. We were proud of him. Then he and his dad got into building model airplanes. They took over one of the bedrooms and spent hours putting them together. The day they took one for its first flight was a very big day. We carefully put it in the car with all the things needed to fly it and headed off to Miracle Mile. The two had worked so hard to put it together, but something went wrong. It took a nosedive straight to the ground! Our hearts sank at the moment of impact. It was back to the drawing board to start all over.

There were other sports that Chuck and Doug did together. They learned to scuba dive, and when we were comfortable that Chuck was ready, we went to Catalina in our boat and they would dive for abalone. They would bring it up from the ocean, we would pound it on the swim-step and throw it in the frying pan, and it was delicious. Norm, Donna, and Doug would come along with their boat and we would have abalone parties. The boys would buzz along in the dinghy and do some waterskiing.

We all went to Mexico on jeeping ventures together with the boys' teachers, who had a home down there. We had some good times down Mexico way, even though Norm was good at getting his jeep stuck!

Norm had eye problems and eventually lost sight in his left eye. He had a heart attack, which affected his life for several years. He then got shingles and was so laid up with pain, he could hardly do anything.

The time came when it was evident he would not make it. He had another heart episode and was admitted to Hoag Hospital. His wife, Donna, called me to see if Ted and I would meet her the next morning; she thought Norm was ready to go home with the Lord.

There was a pastor who went around to rest homes and sang and played his guitar for the elderly folks. His name was Sam Parsons and he was called Singing Sam. He would go in and out of the rooms of those who loved his singing, and many would request his songs. I called him to see if he would join us.

The next morning Ted, our son Chuck, and I went to Hoag Hospital to visit Norm. We were all to meet at 10:00 a.m. with the purpose of singing him to the Lord. When we arrived, we said hello to Norm, who actually looked quite healthy and happy. I said to myself, "There is no way he is ready today. Donna is premature about this." We visited, the doctor came in to check him out, and then the doctor left. Donna went out with the doctor and came back with a small cup of applesauce. Norm always loved to eat.

As it was, Singing Sam was stuck in traffic and was an hour late. Another pastor, Pete Mckensie, arrived, but Ted had to leave to take Chuck to a doctor's appointment. Around 12:00 p.m., Singing Sam arrived with his guitar and we all started singing Christian songs. Sam knew which songs Norm liked, so we had big smiles from Norm.

Donna was by the side of the bed, and then left to go tell the doctor and nurses what we were doing. I stepped up to hold Norm's hand when she left. Pete Mckensie stepped up to the other side of the bed, as it appeared Norm was trying to lift his hands in worship. We lifted his hands over his head for him. Norm seemed to break out in a heavy sweat, so I was rubbing his head to tell him it was okay for him to leave, to release him. He asked where Donna was. I kept rubbing his head, he gave a great big smile, and then he went to Heaven!

Donna returned and went for comfort from Sam. The doctor came in to take Norm's vitals and was in absolute shock that he was gone. What a way to enter Heaven, with all the angels and Jesus standing waiting for him. It was breathtaking to me, especially as I didn't think he was ready! God is so awesome, and he took Norm out of his pain.

One of Norm's eyes was open and when Pastor Pete tried to close it, it wouldn't stay closed. I had to tell him it was because he had a glass eye! Not many knew that Norm had a glass eye, as he hid many of the pains he lived with. He was a happy guy most of the time, even though he lived with shoulder pain from being a pitcher for the Pittsburgh Pirates so many years ago.

Letting go of Norm was bittersweet. But the wonderful thing about those who die as believers is knowing that death is not the end. I am confident that I will see Norm again thanks to the sacrifice Jesus made on the cross so long ago. He opened the way for us to be forgiven from our sins so that we can be together with Him forever after we die.

21

A Time To Hate

I hate disease.

When Chuck was around twenty-six years old, he began acting different—doing weird things. He would imagine bugs coming out of the toilet and crawling under the door. At first, we felt he had taken on too much responsibility: marriage, a new job, a new city, and two new babies. We thought possibly he was having a breakdown. His condition was causing problems in his marriage and all aspects of his life. He went in for an evaluation and the doctors found him to be schizophrenic.

This led to a divorce, which was hard on him— something he never got over. After seven weeks in the hospital, he came to live with us until he got his feet on the ground.

Most of Chuck's time was spent creating and selling pottery. It was a difficult fifteen years together as we tried to find the right medications for him. As soon as a medicine would start to work, he would feel better and stop taking it because the side effects were hard to deal with. For six or seven years, a new medicine worked. He was stable and we had a life again with him. Then again the worst happened. The medicine prescribed began causing diabetes—not just in Chuck, but in all patients who were taking it. It was eventually taken off the market. With that option gone, we were back in the same boat, trying to find a medication that would work.

Chuck had a difficult life trying to follow a diabetic diet, which meant in and out of the hospitals, again and again, for him and us. He lived alone in a trailer park and one night we found him in a diabetic coma. We called 9-1-1 and they took him to the hospital, where he remained in a coma for nine days. On the seventh night, the doctor told us to call his kids, as it was time to pull the plug. We all agreed. As God would have it, someone did not follow instructions and the plug was not pulled. Chuck came out of the coma, and after two more months in the hospital, he was home.

He was never the same. For the next three years, he was angry and had such a different personality. We always felt he was mad at us for calling 9-1-1. He had a death wish.

During this three-year period, he was so hostile to his dad and me that I became angry myself. I still loved him, but I couldn't stand him. Every time I would see him or be involved with him, I would get angrier. He felt the same toward his father and me. He was selfish, not caring how he hurt us. He was just sick.

At a Bible study, there were ladies at my table praying for God to change my heart, change all of our hearts, as we were all angry and impatient. I thought, if I am a Christian, how can I be so angry, so mad—even jealous when Chuck took so much of Ted's time? "Create in me a pure heart, O God, and renew a steadfast spirit within me" (Psalm 51:10 NIV). Ted was always loving and forgiving to Chuck. It was I that felt the guilt more and was crying out to the Lord.

Chuck would have nothing to do with us. He had not been to our house for three years; he was living as a recluse. However, if he needed anything, he was not bashful about asking—he actually expected and acted like we owed him.

Chuck became abusive to the neighbors in the trailer park, so we were asked to move him out. He had lived there for fifteen years, had a great manager, but it was time. He rebelled when we found a place, but he finally settled into the move. The next blow to him was when his longtime friend, his bird, died. It was really difficult on him.

It got to the point where we would give him his daily insulin shots, feed him, give him his pills, do his laundry, etc. He said he couldn't understand why we were still so good to him when he was so bad to us! This was just what we were all praying for—a changed heart.

Ted didn't care to talk about the fact that his son was not normal. We didn't bring it up or share our feelings about it—it was a man thing for him.

Struggling with Chuck—his health, going back and forth to the hospital, two surgeries on his neck from diabetes, two big holes in his neck that we were sure would never heal—we asked God, "Where is the end of this?" We felt so overwhelmed.

One morning I went to his apartment to fix his breakfast. When I opened the door he said, "Hi Mom"! It was like the old Chuck—a complete reversal from his previous behavior! From that point on it was like God washed all the bad memories away—for him and for me. I liked him again; I had compassion for him and we all three felt it. His dad was able to take him to the beach to watch the surfers where he used to surf. They had quality time together, talking about their early days of scuba diving, surfing, and mainly about his relationship with Jesus.

You see, we asked for a change of heart for all three of us in those three months we were so close together. Chuck's heart changed, which caused Ted's and my heart to change. And this is how we were able to say goodbye to Chuck—with love in our hearts and with peace that he is in the Lord's arms. We will see him again one day soon.

When he said, "Hi Mom," it melted my hard heart and all those bad memories left. Sure, they still arise, but we choose to remember our really good years together—our wonderful memories of fun things we did together.

Chuck's children came for the Celebration of Life service, and so did his school buddies, best man, and even some of his friends who had deserted him when his mental illness had gotten so bad. Many of them spoke of their fun times together, what a great guy he was, and the special memories they shared.

Chuck's kids, who had mostly seen him sick, went home with a different picture of their dad. Praise God! They had heard so many negatives, understandably, but this had changed their opinion of him to see what a great dad they had. It's never too late!

We asked Singing Sam, who knew Chuck and Ted from Bible study, to do the eulogy. Sam was able to get Ted to share his feelings about Chuck's problems. It turns out Sam had worked in a mental hospital for five years! God sent him to relieve Ted of holding onto all the pain.

Chuck was like any other kid: he went to school, graduated, married, had kids, and then—wham—got sick. His kids have thanked us for having the service and how much they learned about their father they never knew. That day, I also gave the grandchildren art pieces and jewelry their father made—which they were quite happy to receive.

When we think God is not there for us or we ask, "Where is God when I need Him?" let me tell you that He is taking care of all the details to make the end of our story a blessing. "And we know that for those who love God all things work together for good, for those who are called according to his purpose" (Romans 8:28 ESV).

We can choose to look only at our circumstances, to wallow in hatred, or self-pity, or anger, or frustration. Or we can realize that God is pruning us. We can look at circumstances from a heavenly perspective and choose to put our focus on our eternal home in Heaven. Don't allow Satan to steal your joy; look to Jesus in times of hardship and you will find blessing that only He can give.

22

A Time To Lose

We lost Chuck to the debilitating effects of disease, and we lost Cliff as well. Cliff passed from a heart attack caused by all the meds he was taking for the effects of Agent Orange. Like so many other young men, he had been exposed to the poison in Vietnam, and it shortened his life.

In the normal order of things, parents usually die before their children, so there's something especially sad and difficult about having to bury one's children.

I've buried my parents as well. When they were unable to shovel snow and maintain their life in Big Bear, we brought them down to our ranch house in San Marcos. This was at the same time that we were helping our two sons in business. We had bid on a 155-acre piece of property with a builder and he was going to build seventy houses on it. On the property was a five-bedroom house and two-bedroom caretaker home. We had cleaned up the five-bedroom house and that's what we stayed in during the week when we were working with the kids in their rug businesses.

It was an ideal set-up when we brought my folks down. My dad could fiddle in the yard and do things he liked to do, including cook. Ted and I worked all day and when we came home, dinner was ready, which was great. And in the evenings we had a chance to visit with my folks as adults. Spending time with them like this helped me to wake up and realize all that my parents had gone through together. I began to see my mom in a different light. I was able to lose the negative feelings I had for her and I thanked God for giving me that opportunity to know my real mom, who never had seemed to have time for me. She had heartaches of her own, losing her first daughter to illness and then her first son in the flood.

If I could say anything now to help those who think they have a "bad" mom, or that she doesn't like them, or that they are just a slave to do her work, I would tell them to think about her life from her perspective. Do you think it is a bed of roses? Has she had a lot of joy in her life, a lot of sorrow? Think about how you can help her in her need. We don't all have the opportunity I had to clear the air. That is why God gave us the commandment to honor our mothers and fathers.

I helped my mom for the next sixteen years as she struggled with Alzheimer's, and I don't regret one moment. I can sleep well at night knowing I did my best for her and made her comfortable. And the Lord allowed me to be with her when she left. The same with my dad, who passed away five years before Mom went.

My dad took ill at an extremely difficult time. With Chuck suffering from schizophrenia and my mom sick, I developed shingles on the right side of my face, affecting my eye, teeth, and tongue. When my dad got sick, the doctor ended up giving him too much medication and it was like he went crazy. I went to check him out and he was sitting in the hall trying to thread a needle—but he had no needle or thread. He was a basket case.

Overwhelmed, I remember sitting down and writing a letter to Jesus. The letter included this statement: "Whatever your will is for Dad, I pray it is to take him home." I had brought him to the Lord prior to this, so I was comfortable with him leaving if it was in the Lord's timing. Later that day, my dad passed away. God does answer our prayers and He has been so faithful to me! He allowed me to be with Dad when he left, and I feel confident I will see him again.

I was blessed to say goodbye to both my mom and my dad with no regrets. When the Lord says, "Honor your father and your mother," I can stand in front of Him knowing I did my best.

Being in my nineties, I've experienced the loss not

only of my sons and my parents, but of countless friends and acquaintances who have not survived as long as we have. It's heartbreaking.

We often sit and think about these special people who are no longer in our lives, and we remember the times we had with them.

One of the great promises of the Bible that we cling to is the promise that we will be reunited with our Christian loved ones again who have gone before us to Heaven. Because of what Jesus has done on the cross, He has conquered the grave and death is not the end!

So while we talk about death in terms of "losing someone," in reality, they are not lost and we will still retain our relationship with them. For believers, death is just a delay until we see each other again.

23

A Time To Gain

Cliff and Chuck left us with five wonderful grandchildren. Cliff gave us three grandsons: Callahan, Jeriko, and Kamron. We have had a lot of fun with them as they've grown up. The three boys were raised in Hawaii, so we made many trips to Maui over the years. We would fly Chuck's two kids, Jared and Hillary, out from Missouri to Newport Beach. Then the four of us would fly to Maui. That way, the five grandkids interacted and knew each other over the years.

The boys would go diving to see the beautiful fish that only Hawaii has—things Jared and Hillary had never seen. We would swim in the ocean, the pool, have barbecues and campfires at night, and listen to Hawaiians blow their horns or watch them do the hula for us.

Just recently, we had a reunion in Maui at the same condo on the same beach where we used to go. The "kids" are now grown and have kids of their own (our three great-grandkids) and it was awesome to see their parents taking them to the same places we went. During the reunion, the parents renewed their vows on the beach at sunset, which was very meaningful for all of us.

We've set up a schedule now so that they all come to Newport Beach in the summer and at Christmastime, so we get to see them grow. They all love the beach, paddleboards, building sandcastles, playing at the park—so many things for them to do. I say that the family who plays together stays together. It truly makes for good fellowship.

The five grandchildren and three great-grandchildren that we have from our two sons have given us great pleasure. With our sons gone, we have gone alongside of three grandchildren to take our sons' places, so to speak, to train those old enough how to run a business. It has given us something to do, filling a void for us, and they are learning valuable business skills. Working together in business is a relationship that grandparents and grandchildren normally would not have, so it is a great blessing to interact in this way and to watch them grow their nest eggs. They look forward to coming for business meetings and we love having them.

Despite our loss of Chuck and Cliff, we have gained so much through our relationships with our grandchildren and great-grandchildren. We praise God for the blessing that each one of them is to us.

In addition to all of this, I've also gained a daughter (sort of) named Melissa. This is how. About twenty years ago, my son Cliff wanted to start a rehab for alcoholics in Hawaii. He had lived in Maui raising his three boys on the island and he felt it was necessary to have a rehab facility over there with all the drinking that goes on. Cliff had a problem with drinking himself. So many of the men who were sprayed with Agent Orange in Vietnam became alcoholics, and Cliff was one of them. The war had been vicious on Cliff. Half of his barracks was blown away while he was in Vietnam and he lost so many of his buddies that way.

At the same time that Cliff was recovering and wanting to start a rehab to help other people, Pastor Chuck Smith was trying to buy some property on Molokai to do the same thing. We got together with that goal in mind, and Cliff went to Calvary Ranch for four weeks to learn as much as he could about their program. Then he went to U-Turn for Christ to learn how they do things.

The rehab on Molokai didn't end up happening, but something significant for me came out of the experience. While Cliff was learning at Calvary Ranch in Lakeside, California, we would go there on Sundays and attend church with those who were coming off alcohol and drugs. One Sunday was graduation day for the girls.

They all went forward to kneel and pray as the pastor prayed over them. One cute little blonde caught my heart. I had an angel pin on my blouse so when the girls went back to their seat, I went over and pinned the angel pin on her and said, "If you would like someone to email with and learn more about the Bible, here is my email address." At lunch, she came over and thanked me and said she would like to email.

Her name was Melissa (Missy). We started corresponding and soon we were great friends, writing scriptures and stories back and forth. The following year, Ted and I took the motorhome to visit her in Coeur d'Alene, where she lived. The next year, she got married, and the year after that, she had a baby girl. We started visiting Coeur d'Alene every year to see Melissa, her husband, Chad, and their girl, Alic'n, who was born on the Fourth of July. It was always a fun time of year to see all the fireworks on the lake and visit them and go to church and dinner at the Cedars Floating Restaurant.

Two years later, she had her second daughter, Justice. Melissa's husband started drinking and was in and out of rehab. Their marriage ended in divorce. We kept in touch with Melissa and always went to see her for the Fourth of July.

Melissa remarried a nice fellow named Preston, and a couple years later, they had a son. The girls were delighted with their little brother. Melissa stayed strong in the Lord, memorized the whole book of Revelation, and nobody will sway her away from the love of God. She now goes to Uganda for ten days at a time to help the young kids there find the Lord. We are still close, and she is like the daughter I never had.

Melissa's first daughter, Alic'n, was born with multiple sclerosis, so Melissa had a challenge right from the beginning. Alic'n has had many surgeries to straighten her legs as she grew. They take it all in stride, as part of life. I'm so very proud of all of them and I'm blessed that I gave her the angel pin that day.

24

A Time to Pluck What is Planted

As I look back on my life, I do wonder: if I loved the Lord at an early age like I thought I did, why didn't I follow Him and start working for Him when I was nine or ten years old? I think He gives us time to go through His experiences to teach us how to respond to trials and adversity.

"Yet, so many years were wasted," I sometimes think. But God tells us in His Word that He will make up all the time that has been wasted.

> *I will restore to you the years that the*
> *swarming locust has eaten,*
> *The crawling locust,*
> *The consuming locust,*
> *And the chewing locust,*
> *My great army which I sent among you.*
> *You shall eat in plenty and be satisfied,*
> *And praise the name of the Lord your*

God, Who has dealt wondrously with you;
And My people shall never be put to
shame.

- Joel 2:25–26

In our case, He really did make up the time that was wasted! It was not till the 1980s that we became born again and gave Him everything we owned. It's His; He gave it to us and we gave it back. The more we gave to Him, the more He showered on us. If we invested in a property, when we sold it, we had an awesome return. Yes, we made mistakes along the way, but it was also a learning lesson.

I mentioned we came back from our honeymoon and dove right into the rug cleaning business. We were in the LA area and as time went by, other rug cleaners were having trouble and we bought them out, so we were expanding quite well. That is, until the Watts riot came about. We were right in the middle of it. Rioters shot our friend up the street, held up the dry cleaners across the street, and that night, Ted said, "It's time to move out of the area."

The same night at 3:00 in the morning, our friend Norm called us to say, "You need to buy my house. You are down here every weekend anyway, so how about it?" Had Norm been a drinker, we would have thought he was drunk.

Norm had bought another home, had not sold his house, and couldn't make two payments. He gave us a price and we bought it right then. We moved in the next week. We sold our carpet cleaning business and our house and were thinking of retiring. We gave retirement a try, but Ted was only forty-one and too young.

Ted started a car tune-up business, but within a year, he was bored and started doing a couple of rugs a week in our garage. It wasn't long until we had too many rugs to clean so we rented a little shop on 17th Street in Costa Mesa and Ted was the one who introduced steam cleaning to Orange County. We bought two steam-cleaning machines and away we went. Before long, business was booming.

The office girl we had employed in LA had moved to Orange County, so we hired her again to help in the office. Eventually, we sold the business to her and her husband. He was in the army with Ted, they had six kids, and he was working for the phone company. We gave them South County and we kept North County, working all of it out of one building.

As time went by, Ted wanted to get into real estate, so we sold the carpet cleaning business to them and that family is still running it. It was always good to us as far as making a living, but it was time to move on.

This was in the '60s and '70s. Ted had gone into a roofing business on the side, when we were in LA, with a school buddy and they did very well with it. But now he wanted to try probates. We would bid in court for the property; the judge would let us buy it and start fixing it up because we were putting money into it and it wasn't empty that way. We would buy the house, fix it up with a crew, and put it on the market for sale. One year, we did twenty-two houses! We were going along well, doing that for a while, and rolling the houses into property we could build apartments on. We got very involved in the Huntington Beach area with a young builder partner and we built apartment houses. Next, we rolled them into condos; however, they were a lot of work, so we traded the condos for industrial buildings in San Marcos.

Ted was one who "never let the grass grow under his feet." He was always busy and into things—upgrading, coming up with better ways to do the rug cleaning, looking for opportunities. He was gifted that way! So there was never a dull moment in our life, and we made a great team working together.

After the industrial buildings, we got into commercial buildings with Tower Records and Carl's Jr. We found these to be easier—no "hands on" work to speak of. The tenants would take care of all the maintenance and repairs and we just collected the rent.

A few years ago, a realtor came to us to tell us we only had six years left on our Carl's Jr. lease and that it would be a good time to do a 1031 exchange if we sold it now. (This type of transaction defers taxes if you use the profits from the sale to purchase a property of a similar kind.) If we waited much longer, it would be harder to sell with a short-term lease. Prices were up, and the property was worth twice what we thought it was. We went forward and ended up with three ground leases and we find them to be even better than owning commercial. There is little you have to do.

As we retire, we have few worries, as they are all triple-net leases, which means the tenants take care of all of the additional expense such as insurance, maintenance, and property taxes.

God has honored and blessed all of the work we put in over the years with a bountiful harvest, both monetary and spiritual. We find that as we give it all back to Him, it multiplies and produces more and more fruit.

A Time To Tear

After we were empty nesters, we traveled to many different places. While in Holland, we visited Ted's cousin, whose son Paul was soon graduating. They were trying to figure out where to send him for college. We told them he could come live with us and go to Orange Coast for a year and see how he liked it.

In September 1975, he came to live with us. It was a great experience. This young man was good looking, spoke five languages, had a cute accent and everything the girls here liked. Within a week of school starting, the phone rang off the hook and we heard, "Is Paul there?"

He stayed the whole year, then got a roommate and they moved into an apartment of their own. They both went on to Cal State Fullerton and both graduated together. Paul ended up with his master's degree and became a doctor of Sports Medicine and was chosen to run the tennis team at Key Biscayne, Florida, for nineteen years. He has also written two books on tennis.

Paul had a professor named Ron Rietveld who had been at Fullerton quite a while. He took a liking to Paul and they became buddies. Another person who came from Holland and ended up near Fullerton was Corrie ten Boom. You may be familiar with the book or the movie *The Hiding Place*, which tells the story of the ten Boom family, who were clockmakers that owned a shop in Haarlem, Holland. During the war when the Jews were not safe in the streets, Corrie's family put up a fake wall in an upper room and hid many Jews from the Gestapo behind that wall. Corrie and her family saved many lives that way.

Eventually, they were caught and sent to a concentration camp, where the father, Casper, died. Corrie and her sister Betsie were able to get a smuggled Bible and shared its precious truth with many inside the camp. Betsie died in the concentration camp and as the war ended, Corrie was released on a technicality. She became a self-proclaimed "tramp for the Lord," traveling and speaking all over the world. She ended up in a little house near Fullerton, where she became bedridden.

Corrie was a friend of Professor Ron. They had known each other in Holland. Professor Ron came to Paul one day and asked him if he could translate Corrie's notes so they could finish the book she had been writing. I tell this story because what are the chances of that happening? Things don't just happen by accident; they are orchestrated by the Lord. Had Paul not come to live with us or if Corrie had ended up in some other town, this wouldn't have happened! And it was Corrie's meeting with Paul that caused him to come into a personal relationship with the Lord.

After Paul, his wife, and their son had moved to Florida, Ted and I decided to take a motorhome trip to visit them there. We were not aware of his meeting with Corrie ten Boom, but while we visited them, Corrie's name came up because I was reading *The Hiding Place*. He showed me all of her books he had collected and then told me to look up on the wall. Hanging there was a needlepoint that read, "Jesus is Victor" and it was done by Corrie, who took a liking to Paul and wanted them to have it for his help in finishing her book. In her book *A Tramp for the Lord* is a picture of this framed needlepoint that she gave to Paul.

One particular episode from Corrie's life has struck a chord with me, and it centers on the topic of forgiveness. Years after she had been released from the concentration camp and was traveling the world to tell others about Jesus, a man came up to speak with her after one of her talks. She recognized him as an officer from the concentration camp where she and her sister had been so brutally treated. The man had become a Christian and had received the Lord's forgiveness, but he also wanted to ask forgiveness from Corrie, and he extended a hand to her.

In the few seconds that it took for her to make a decision, all of the pain and anger and heartache from that horrible time came rushing back to her and she had to silently ask the Lord to provide her with His forgiveness because she couldn't muster any of her own. The Lord gave her His love and forgiveness for that man, and she was genuinely able to shake his hand with true humility and compassion. God had provided the forgiveness she needed.

That lesson was particularly valuable to me in relation to my ex-husband, John L.

I had had little to no contact with John L. since our divorce, until the day of Cliff's funeral. John L., of course, had every right to be there as he was Cliff's father, but I worried about what our meeting would look like. Ted reassured me that it would all turn out all right.

Thanks to the Lord, my meeting with John L. that day was without feelings of animosity, anger, or hurt. After the funeral, John L. contacted me about giving me some of Cliff's things that were in his possession, so we met again. I was a little surprised when, at that meeting, John L. said that he wanted to change subjects and not talk about Cliff, but instead talk about church and God.

Now here's the thing: Why should someone in my

position care about my ex-husband or his spiritual state? After the things he had done to me, who would blame me if I didn't reach out with the Good News? But thanks be to God—He allowed me to share the gospel with John L. and He gave me a concern for his soul. God tells us that in order to receive forgiveness, we must first forgive others, and I certainly didn't want anything to stand in the way of fully receiving God's forgiveness in my life.

Looking back, I can see how John L.'s early life and circumstances were not easy. He spent forty-four months in Iwo Jima, going into the Marines when he was seventeen years old because his dad had signed for him. He and his brothers all went into the service together. Within four months of getting out, we married, so he had no time to really relax and process what he had been through. These things do not excuse his behavior but I can see that it was a big mistake for us to jump into marriage so quickly. It's important to really get to know someone before marrying them.

Anyway, I was able to share with John L. the contents of a gospel tract, and even asked him if he wanted to pray the prayer of acceptance that was written at the end. John L. declined, saying he wanted to think about it some more, but God gave me the boldness to ask, "What if this is your last opportunity? What if you were in an accident on the way home and didn't have another chance to get right with the Lord?"

John L. still declined, but guess what happened on his drive home? He was in a terrible accident and his car flipped five times. As he hung from his seatbelt upside down in that car, guess what he was thinking about?

Several times after that incident, John L. would send me religious literature that he had received, to ask me about it. Most of it was not biblical, and I would tell him so. I sent him a Bible and he was delighted to get it and would often call to talk about what he was reading. One day, on the phone, I asked him again if he wanted to pray the prayer at the end of the gospel tract and he said that God could never forgive someone like him. We talked and I showed him scriptures where Jesus paid for all of our sins and would forgive him if he just asked the Lord and meant it with all of his heart. Knowing what a con man John L. was, I told him that he couldn't con God and he had to be sincere. Then John L. agreed to pray the prayer to accept the Lord.

Now, John L. has always been a con man, and my guard has always been up with him, never knowing if he is genuine or if he is just saying what I want to hear in order to "keep the door open," so to speak. So I have never been quite sure about if he was sincere in his decision to invite God into his heart and life, but I truly hope so and rest in the fact that I did my part to lead him to the truth.

I call this chapter "A Time to Tear" because there is

a tearing away that comes with forgiving someone. You have to tear out from your heart the feelings of pride, resentment, retaliation, anger, and frustration, and you have to give those things over to the Lord. He will supply you with the forgiveness and love that you need to extend to those who have hurt you.

26

A Time To Heal

Ted and I have always enjoyed very good health, hardly even suffering from the occasional cold. But not too long ago, I was in the hospital for two weeks, followed by time in a rehabilitation center. They treated me for pneumonia.

Unfortunately, the medication they gave me was a newer medication, and they have since found that in certain people it causes the growth of a type of fungus.

Apparently, I am one of those people, and it caused my chest to feel like it was on fire. I couldn't eat anything but malted milkshakes. (Ted, not letting anything go to waste and not having me home to cook for him, helped himself to the breakfast provided by the rehab facility since I was not able to eat it!)

Even though I still was quite sick with this fungus, they discharged me from the rehab place. Thankfully, I had a follow-up appointment with my doctor the following week. When I told him that I was not able to eat anything, was losing weight, and was burning up inside, he examined my tongue and saw that I had the fungal infection. The doctor prescribed a chalky drink four times a day and thankfully, the fungus abated and finally was gone.

We later came to find out that a pastor friend of ours in Dallas, Texas, was given the same medication after taking chemo for cancer. Three days later, he died from the fungus.

I feel that if I hadn't had that doctor's appointment and had allowed the fungus to go unchecked, I probably wouldn't be here to tell this story!

We serve a God who heals—sometimes through doctors and medicine, other times supernaturally through miraculous healings. And He does not only heal physically, but mentally and spiritually as well. So I encourage you to call out to Him if you are suffering or are unwell and ask Him to heal you. He loves to give good gifts to His children.

27

A Time to Gather Stones Together

On one of our motorhome trips many years ago, we were traveling to the East Coast and had stopped someplace in Texas at a laundromat to wash our clothes. There was a bookcase where people could drop off books and, if they saw one they liked, they could take it. "Pretty nice," I thought.

By that time, I had been born again so I was passing out 365-day Bibles and had other books to share. I saw *God's Smuggler*, written by Brother Andrew, and it piqued my interest, so I traded for it and took it along with us on the trip. Ted and I read it, and we were intrigued with how Brother Andrew smuggled Bibles into the countries where Bibles were scarce. I became very interested in his work, got on his ministry's mailing list, and became a donor. We have met Brother Andrew personally and are still involved with his ministry.

I bring this up to say, things that can seem coincidental or even insignificant—like picking up a random book in a laundromat—are not by accident. Without a doubt, the Lord orchestrates the circumstances and details of the lives of His children.

A little later on, I heard of Chuck Colson, who was under President Nixon during Watergate. Chuck did a wrong, was caught, and went to jail, where he found the Lord. When he got out, he started a ministry called Prison Fellowship, helping the prisoners and their children. That struck a chord with me since my ex-husband had been in jail and I thought of all the children who didn't have their dad or mom and couldn't afford Christmas toys or even food.

From time to time, I remembered how hard it was for me to make ends meet with my son. So I got on the Prison Fellowship mailing list and became a donor and am still involved with what they call Angel Tree, their program that helps prisoners send Christmas presents to their kids.

In 1990, I broke my ankle, so I was laid up for a while. During that time, I had begun to listen to Christian radio stations, and that's how I heard the story of Joni, who at age seventeen dove into a lake, hit her head on the bottom, and instantly became a quadriplegic. What a story!

On the radio, I heard Joni say she was going to be in Brea and she was signing books for Christmas. I said to myself, "I have to go and meet her!" I did, and she was signing books with her pen in her mouth. I had bought sixteen books for gifts and she said she would sign them all! When I saw the effort she went to in signing them, I felt so bad that I had bought so many books. She was delighted and said, "That's what I do!" Oh my, what an example of patience and grace!

Joni and I became longtime friends and I did two fundraisers at our house for her organization. When her need outgrew the room at my house, we helped her get into churches. Pastor Chuck Smith was someone I went to, and he opened up the Murrieta Hot Springs Conference Center for her.

The Lord put an urge in me to want to bring the message of salvation to everyone who didn't know Jesus. Campus Crusade for Christ, an organization out of San Bernardino (Arrowhead Springs) was advertising the *Jesus* film on the radio. I looked them up, read about them, and mentioned to Ted that I was interested in getting involved.

We had a cabin in Big Bear so he said, "Let's stop by and see what kind of an office they have when we go home to Newport." When we got there, Paul Eshelman, who was directing the film project, happened to be there. He showed us all around, and we got to see how they made the movie, and how they were showing it to people all around the world. In some countries it was simply projected onto a large white sheet using a generator in the middle of nowhere. But because of the power of the gospel message, many people responded, giving their lives to the Lord simply through watching the film. We got involved with them as well, even giving the videos out door-to-door.

When we first became "on fire" to learn more about the Bible and were traveling in our motorhome, we had heard several radio programs by Pastor David Jeremiah, so we ordered several of his sets of teachings and we listened to them from California to Florida and back. We liked them so well, we ordered more and started passing them around after we had listened to them. We later invited him to The Cannery Restaurant with Pastor Jerry Wear and, oh, how he liked their crab cakes! They were so good, we ordered more for him to take home to his wife, Donna.

At a later time, Dr. J (as he said we could call him) came to the house for a visit. We feel we learned so much from him in our early days as Christians—and in so much detail!

Eventually, I became friends with a waitress at Mimi's, a restaurant where we went early in the morning for breakfast. She was another one who wanted to spread the Word. I would give the tapes to her and she would loan them to those she was ministering to, like a lending library. I would supply her with new ones and we had a regular ministry going on. You would be surprised how many people were open to hearing the Word in this way.

Another ministry that has impacted us is that of Josh and Dottie McDowell. They are soldiers for the Lord and are under Campus Crusade for Christ. Josh teaches all over the world, spreading the Word. He has several books that tell the story of the gospel in different ways, including *The Witness* and *More than a Carpenter*.

Other organizations that moved us to support their missions were J. Vernon McGee's Thru the Bible radio ministry, Zola Levitt Ministries, and On Wings of Eagles, which helps to bring Jews back to their land of Israel. I was first drawn to their ministry because of a billboard that quoted Isaiah 40:31, which says that those who wait on the Lord will "mount up with wings like eagles." This reminded me of my dad's eagle and sparked my interest.

Eventually, we left the church we were in for fifteen years and started attending Calvary Chapel with Pastor Chuck Smith. He was well known for starting his ministry for the hippies in a tent. We liked his presentation and the way he explained the Bible.

While Ted was in the army, he was a radio technician, so when we got better acquainted with Pastor Chuck and he was getting involved with radio stations, Ted said, "What a great way to get the Word out, and when we go to Heaven, it will still be going." We made an appointment with Pastor Chuck and told him we were interested in getting involved. He liked the idea and his goal for that year was to have a hundred stations. I think he ended up with more than two hundred, and we just kept going!

Ted was in a Bible study where a group wanted to build a church in Romania, and also one in Uganda. We were able to get involved with those projects and what a thrill it was the day the doors opened! The one in Uganda had an orphanage for children who lost their parents to AIDS. We had five hundred little mouths to feed, bodies to clothe, and beds to fill.

I say all this not to brag of what we did, but to brag on what the Lord did through us. It has been an awesome, fulfilling experience and it continues on and on. The more the Lord puts on our hearts, the more funds He sends our way so we can do His work. And there is so much more work to do!

We have recently become involved with Harvest Ministries in their crusades. We feel time is running out and there are so many unsaved souls. Crusade-style evangelism, like Billy Graham used to do, is an effective way to bring many people into God's kingdom. Pastor Greg Laurie does a wonderful job with these crusades. A few years ago, they held the largest single-day evangelistic event ever to take place in America, right in Dallas, Texas. They filled up AT&T Stadium and had to close the doors and turn people away. Many thousands of people came forward at the event to accept Christ.

Ministries like these reflect where our hearts are: we've been commissioned to tell the world the Good News of Jesus Christ and we feel that our time is running out and the need is great to bring into the kingdom as many as we can, while we can. There's a saying that goes, "You can't take it with you, but you can send it on ahead by using your resources for the Lord's work," and that's true.

In Joshua 4, after the children of Israel had passed through the Jordan River, God instructed the people to take twelve stones from the riverbed and set them up as a monument, to remind future generations of the great things God had done for them. In some ways, I feel that each of these ministries that we've been able to support is like a stone. Together they form an altar of worship, as well as a monument— not to the glory of Ted and Geneva Servais, but to the glory of God. And when future generations are blessed by the work of these ministries, God will be glorified! That's the kind of legacy we want to leave.

A Time to Die

As Ted and I live out our "golden years" and we reminisce about all the things we have done together, it's hard to believe what a full life we have had.

Ted was always into trying new things. At one point, we went to school to learn the rules for operating ham radios, just like my dad used to do. We joined a club for ham radio operators and before long, we were talking to folks all over the world. You've already heard about our skiing, flying, and motorhoming. We were always keeping busy. Why, for a time we were even into motorcycling. Ted's handle was "Big Foot" and I was "Honda Mama"!

We have been blessed with good health, so the Lord has been able to accomplish much in our lives. We have had very few sick days in fifty-seven years of marriage, and we don't take that lightly. So many of our friends have had cancer or passed away. We have kept a good diet and exercised through tennis and other sports. I believe that keeping active, as well as reading and writing, has kept my mind from dementia. But it is more than that.

When you buy a new car or piece of equipment, it comes with a manual that has "how to" instructions. It is the same with life. God has given us a manual, a book of instructions for how to live. It is the Bible. The Lord never said that life would be a bed of roses. In fact, He told us there would be hard times. There would be mountains to climb and then valleys to traverse, but He calls us to follow Him and He promises He will never leave us or forsake us.

Our life has been a great example of that. We have had hardships and heartaches—and we have had oh so many fun times as well. We have traveled the world and seen so many things that others have never even heard of, such as Palau in the Caroline Islands, where the native men have tattoos from head to toe and their wives go topless. We've seen war zones where airplanes dove into the ground and are still there. We've seen beautiful spots like Lake Louise in Banff National Park and flown over the tops of the Alps in a little airplane.

On one trip with our carpet cleaner colleagues, we got to go to Switzerland, Holland, Norway, Italy, and more. We went to Germany and saw Hitler's cave underground where he built the airplanes in secret. They had opened it up again and let water in, so we went in by boat. We then visited the "Eagle's Nest," a great location in the rocks where he could see anyone approaching.

We then went on to Scotland and Ireland and saw so much beauty. (But nothing was as beautiful as where we live right now in Newport Beach.)

Yes, we worked hard, followed our goals, and accomplished much as we listened to the lead of our Lord. The best years of our lives have been since we submitted it all to Him; from that point on, I can't even put in words what awesome things He has done through us because we were open and listening to Him.

God has a job for each of us; we each have a purpose in life. Some are givers, others are doctors, nurses, volunteers, pastors—such a wide variety of jobs. When you find what you think your passion is, then go for it. Ask Him to guide you and you will be amazed at what happens. Pray on it. Just talk to Him, which was one thing I didn't know how to do early on.

Once I got on my knees and asked Him into my heart, there was no question what I was to do or where I was going. Although Ted and his first wife were baptized and they dedicated their business to the Lord, once she passed away, he got away from it as he grieved. Then we married, and you've heard the rest of the story.

There is no question in my mind it was the work of the Lord that the investments we made increased so much in value so that we could gift it back to the Lord's work.

As we look at the world today, as upside down as it seems to be, when we read the Bible, we are right on schedule! I believe we are very close to the Lord's return. When they start saying "peace and safety," we can know that that our redemption is near. So as I see it, we have little time to do His work.

Instead of trying to build an empire here in the world, find something you can do for Him and build your home in Heaven. He says that whatever you do on earth, He will reward you for it in Heaven. So send it on ahead and be ready to have Him say, "Well done, My good and faithful servant."

You must be born again (see John 3:3), so do that first and He will take care of the rest.

When I look back, if I had to do it over again, I wouldn't change anything. We needed to go through the hardships so we could help others go through them too. And the blessings we've received as a result have made it all worth it.

I pray this book has somehow helped you. My goal was to share my life in the hope it would help others cope, and help them to find the Lord at an earlier age than I did.

If you have never prayed to receive Jesus into your life as Lord and Savior, I encourage you to do so right now. You can have the forgiveness of your sins, abundant life here on earth, and the promise of Heaven when you die. All you have to do is believe that Jesus sacrificed His life to save you, turn from your sinful ways, and live your life in obedience to Him. You can pray a prayer like the one below, and as long as you are sincere, Jesus will come into your heart and life to be your Father, Savior, and Friend.

> *Jesus, I ask You to forgive me of my sins and be the Ruler of my heart from now on. I turn from my sinful ways and want to follow You instead. Help me to do that. Thank You for dying on the cross on my behalf so that I can have the hope of eternal life in Heaven. I ask You to be my Lord and my Savior. I give my life back to You now. Amen.*

If you prayed that prayer and meant it from your heart, you can know that God has accepted you into His family and you can have the assurance that you will go to Heaven when you die. I encourage you to learn more about what it means to start following Jesus at KnowGod.org. I can't imagine what the next season in my life will hold, but I know that the Lord will be right beside me. Reader, will you join me for the ride as we follow the Lord together?

Acknowledgements

I want to thank my husband for being patient while I wrote this book, as it took precious time away in our late years of life for me to complete it. It is a story that could never be written if he had not asked me to marry him. He is the assertive one who made most of these stories happen. I could never have picked a better person to love, partner with, and befriend. After fifty-seven years of marriage (plus three years of dating), we still love each other, kiss each other, tell one another, "I love you," and want to spend valuable time together while we can. Thank you, Ted, for a great life together.

To my Bible study ladies at my table: Marla Toomire, Karen Meguiar, Susan Milhand, Susan Scott, Cindy Allen, Charlotte Carlson, Myrna Petersen, Connie Maris, Mia Megan, Sandy Mazy, Carol Vanion, Virginia Olson, and so many more—I give thanks for what I have learned from each one of you.

Marla Toomire has been at the same table with me for some twenty-five years. She is so knowledgeable and a good leader who helps me as a friend when I am sick and will do anything for me. Thank you.

To my leader, Kim Kaptor and coleader, Dawn Smith. You were encouragers who have called my stories "little nuggets" that others can learn lessons from. Dawn is so young to know all that she shares and she loves the Lord. She is a prayer warrior as well.

To Brian and Cheryl Brodersen. Cheryl has heard some of my stories and asked if I would give my testimony on video for her ladies' Bible study. I have done two with her. Her husband took Pastor Chuck Smith's place when he passed and he is getting better every day. He also is going through the Bible and we can understand him the way he does it.

To Laura Jackson and Linda, such faithful ones for Calvary.

To Chris Camden, who answered my call when I wanted to know more about Harvest Ministries and Pastor Greg Laurie. He met with Ted and me and gave us all the information we wanted, and he bends over backward to help us. Thank you, Chris and Carolyn.

Chris introduced us to Rex and Diane Jackson, who hosted and escorted us around Dallas for the Harvest America event, where so many people came to Christ in Texas and all over the world. We bonded immediately with Rex and Diane and have stayed in contact ever since.

To the Jacksons' son Brian, who helped put this book together. I had said no to Brian in the beginning, but he followed God's lead in outlining the chapters to fit Ecclesiastes 3 and I am so pleased with it as it came out just as I had envisioned it to be. I am thankful for the effort he put into it.

To Carol Timmons, my friend of many years. I treasure her input when we get together. She has often said, "Geneva, you may want to write a book." She has heard my testimony and felt others might be helped by my experiences. She has been my encourager, and when I sent her a draft for her opinion, she agreed with me that it is just what it should be. I was very encouraged by that as she has such knowledge and experience. She also called me one night to say, "Let's claim Psalm 71:18-21," which can be found at the beginning of this book.

And, oh, my Joni Tada, who has been such a model to follow. She is one who has been through so much real pain daily for decades, but keeps on smiling and pursuing her goals for the disabled. Her thirty-seven-year marriage is so strong, with Ken working right alongside of her. I have a date with Joni when we both get on the other side to fly kites together—something we both did with our dads with a fishing pole! She will dance with her Ken and with her King—no braces and the freedom to move freely.

To Cindy Shrey, who was my heart-to-heart partner for five years. We met once a week to pray for each other's family and to encourage one another in our daily struggles. We met for early breakfast as well as at the ladies' retreats in Arrowhead Springs.

To Dolly Carlson, who at a retreat at Murrieta Hot

Springs, picked me out of all of her ladies and gave me a very nice compliment, thank you.

To Judy and Joel Slutsky, our special neighbors for forty-three years! We have had the best relationship a family could ask for. In all those years, we have never had even one issue with each other, which proves to me we can all have different beliefs, friends, lives, and ideas, and still live in peace with others. Thank you for letting us watch you raise your family, for the matzo ball soup, and the holiday dinners.

To Liz (my nail gal), who has been my friend for forty-five years!

To my prayer warriors: Peggy and Phil Twente, Daniel C., and Diana H. Thank you for praying!

To so many ministry leaders and representatives who have helped to shape our knowledge of Christ and allowed us to partner with them in the Lord's work, many who have already been mentioned in this book: Chuck and Kay Smith, David and Gwen Wilkerson, Bill and Vonette Bright, Kathleen Albright, Jerry and Emma Wear, Paul and Kathy Eshelman, Steve and Judy Douglas, Larry Buck, David and Donna Jeremiah, Josh and Dottie McDowell, Kay Arthur, James and Shirley Dobson, Brother Andrew, Greg and Cathe Laurie, and so many more. Thank you for your influence and impact on my life.

Geneva's dad, Ted Ducey, circa 1940

Geneva's parents, Ted and Geneva, celebrating their 50th anniversary

Geneva and her sister Drusilla as children

Geneva and her sister Drusilla as children

Geneva and her sister Drusilla as children

Geneva and her sister Drusilla as children

Geneva (right) and her sister Drusilla as children

Geneva and Drusilla

The Ducey Children: Geneva, Teddy, Jerry, Drusilla — 1937

Geneva as a cheerleader

Geneva (left) in a singing trio

Geneva (second to left) in a singing quintet

The Nysaean Singers, Geneva third from left, bottom row

Geneva's pin as President of the Nysaean Singers

Music was always a major part of Geneva's life,
photo circa 1943

Geneva and brother Ted, 1945

Ted Servais, 1956

Ted Servais, graduation, 1947

Ted and his first wife, Joanne, October 28, 1952

Salton Sea Races, circa 1955

Cashier of the Month

Cashier of the Month for November is Geneva Welsh. She received the honor while still a cashier at the Encino store. Recently she was named head cashier at Woodman.

Geneva is beginning her fifth year with Ralphs. She started with the company as a cashier at Reseda. Her success as a cashier, plus her selection as a Cashier of the Month and her recent promotion, is credited to her exceptional abilities and pleasing manner. Geneva has done a wonderful job as a cashier, and she is expected to uphold her former standards in her new position.

Geneva, her husband, John, and son Clifford, 12, live in Northridge. All are water ski enthusiasts. Geneva has won eight trophies in water ski races sponsored by the Los Angeles Ski Club, of which she is a member. Two years ago she made a round tip to Catalina on skis, a grueling task which took almost three hours.

Cashier of the Month, circa 1955

Geneva's badge and pin from working at Ralphs

1958 Mercury Mustang ski boat.
The boat that brought Ted and Geneva together.

Longtime friends Norm and Donna Carpenter with Ted and Geneva

Geneva and son Clifford, circa 1955

Wedding photo, April 8, 1962

Geneva and Ted's wedding day, with Cliff and Chuck

Ted and Geneva on their honeymoon

Chuck enjoying scuba diving

Ted waterskiing, 1960

Chuck waterskiing

Geneva in Catalina

Geneva's brother, Ted Ducey Jr, who was lost in the flood

Ted and Geneva's home away from home

Geneva's son Clifford in Sheriff's uniform

Clifford's family, 1990

Cliff's children: Jeriko, Kameron, and Callahan

Jeriko and Kameron

One of the Servaises' planes

Chuck as an adult

Geneva and her son Cliff, 2001

Ted and "Singing Sam", 2010

Melissa (Missy), who received the angel pin from Geneva

Ted's Dutch nephew Paul, Paul's wife Barbara, and their son Daniel

Chuck's children: Jared and Hillary

The cabin in Big Bear, named "The Eagles' Nest"

Women's Bible study group

*Great-grandchildren Cameron, Quinn, and Charlotte with their parents,
Jared and Hannah*

Geneva and her first husband, John L., 2019

Geneva and Ted, circa 1999